@ Steven J Bradley 2025

Steven J Bradley has asserted his right under the Copyright Designs and Patents Act 1988 to be identified as the author of this work, Deadly Obsessions, The Seduction of Speed.

All rights reserved. No part of this publication may be reproduced or transmitted in any form or by any means, Electronic, or mechanical, including photocopying, recording, or any information storage or retrieval system, without prior permission in writing from the publisher

ISBN. 9798897984084

DEADLY OBSESSIONS

Part one
The Seduction of Speed

STEVE BRADLEY

Brooklands Members Banking ... ghosts walk here.

Introduction:
The Birth and Early Development of Motor Sport

Until 1895, every motorist had to follow a walking man who would wave a red flag to warn the population that a mechanical monster was approaching.

The repeal of the Red Flag Act in 1896 paved the way for speed to become the 20th century addiction. The sound, smell and the sensation of it would drive and define the lives of a certain type of people regardless of their perceived class or with determination, even wealth.

In 1895 the first organised motor race took place in France over public roads between Paris and Bordeaux, won by Emile Levassor with his Panhard Levassor driven at a top speed of 18.5mph. These early French races were all run on public roads and by the turn of the century top speeds of more than 50mph were achieved. Thousands of people would gather to watch these roaring, smoking machines thunder past, usually in clouds of smoke and eye stinging dust.

By 1903 speeds had increased and were now reaching 100mph. The cars had become too fast for the open public roads. Extremely poor road surface conditions, animals and people wandering onto the narrow roads and lack of visibility in the dust storms which followed each cars progress made it "Russian roulette at 90mph" as one contemporary driver described it.

The almost inevitable disaster happened in the Paris to Madrid race before the cars had even reached halfway.

Two drivers, a mechanic and five spectators were killed in crashes. The race was stopped and racing on open public roads came to an immediate end.

In England, no "racing," would be allowed by law for another two years, but to celebrate the repeal of the red flag act, the Motor Car Club organized a run between London and Brighton. This event still carries on to this day.

The first car race on British soil, the Tourist Trophy in 1905 held on the Isle of Man. This, won by J Napier driving an Arrol-Johnson averaging 33.9mph, attracted 42 starters. The Isle of Man didn't have the 20mph speed limit enforced everywhere else in Great Britain so the Manx Government could close roads whenever they wanted.

With the building of the 3.75-mile Brooklands track by Hugh Locke-King in 1907, which became known as "The Birthplace of British Motor Racing", Britain had its first permanent motor racing circuit. It gave drivers and public their first opportunity to watch cars driven at speed without having to travel overseas for the experience.

With typical English eccentricity, Brooklands organized their races using rules and ideas from the horse racing world. The first meeting held on 6th July 1907 heralded as "a motor Ascot".

Until 1914 the drivers wore coloured jackets rather than having numbers on their cars, bookmakers were allowed at Brooklands and cars handicapped as in horse racing. Entry prices for the public enclosures were set high to ensure the Brooklands motto of "The right crowd and no crowding" This approach would prevail throughout the track's existence.

The development of motorcycles gave the less affluent a chance to experience the thrill of speed.

Numerous young men began their speed addiction in

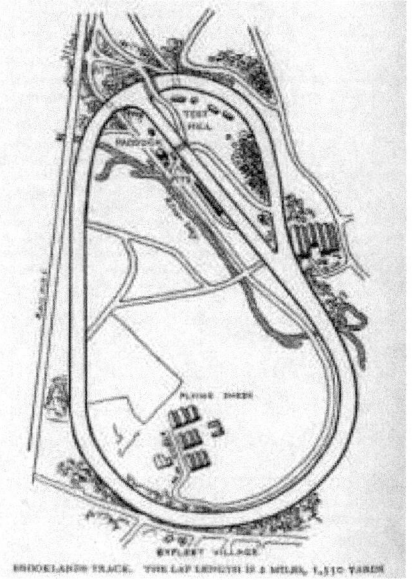

this way, and through their start in motorcycle racing. The best became extraordinarily successful and went on to be famous racing drivers.

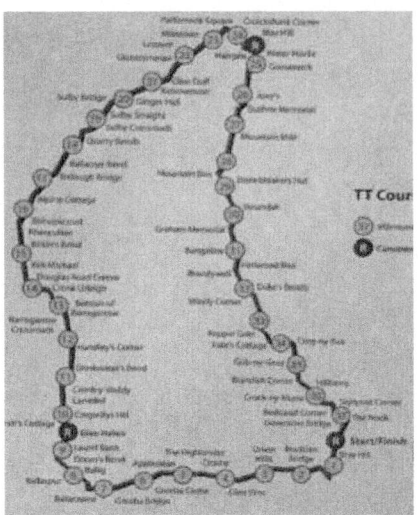

In 1907as England constructed the concert bowl of Brooklands from marsh and woodland in Surrey, the Isle of Man was chosen to host the first major motorcycle race in a Great Britain. For the first four years a "short" course was used as early motorcycles were single-gear, belt-drive models which could not climb the mountain section of the course. Since 1911 the narrow 37-mile course has remained unchanged to his day. The TT races considered to be the most challenging and dangerous motorcycle races in the world.

In Europe racing developed quicker than in England, using closed public roads, and it gave Italy and France the opportunity to become the leading manufacturers of racing cars. In 1906 France organised the first Grand Prix at Le Mans.

This was not the circuit to be made famous in the 1920's but one using a 64-mile lap on the lanes and dusty roads around the city. Hungarian driver

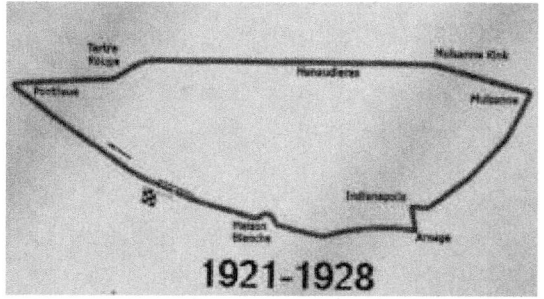

1921-1928

Ferenc Szisz won by driving a cherry red 12.9 litre Renault averaging 62.9mph. Renault had fitted the new development of Michelin detachable rims, which gave them considerable advantage. The poor condition of the roads caused punctures, the scourge of these early races.

Szisz is a good example of the opportunities the birth of motor sport offered young men at the turn of the century. An engineer in Hungary he moved to Paris and joined Renault in 1900. He became riding mechanic for Marcel Renault, tragically Marcel died in the 1903 Paris-Madrid race, and his brother Louis Renault promoted Szisz to driver.

With his win in the 1906 race, he became a Hungarian hero.

Also, in 1906, held for the first time in Italy, was the famous road race the Targa Florio around the bandit-ridden Sicilian roads. The initial race, run over three laps of the islands 92.47-mile circuit. Alessandro Cagno won driving an Itala.

Cagno, like Szisz, came from a working-class background. He became an apprentice engineer and his passion for mechanics saw him become the third employee of FIAT. He also started as a riding mechanic, taking part in the ill-fated Paris-Madrid race.

His driving ability saw Cagno promoted to racing driver and in 1906 he joined another famous Turin manufacturer Itala for whom he won races including at first Targa Florio.

The skill and daring of these flamboyant characters produced the first super stars of motor racing, one of the best being Felice Nazzaro the son of a Turin coal merchant. Nazzaro was said to "handle a car like a violin". One of his greatest young fans was Enzo Ferrari.

The Peugeot Grand Prix cars of 1912 were to revolutionize engine development with their overhead valves and twin overhead camshafts. They won the 1912 French Grand Prix and set the general layout for all future racing engines.

1914 would bring the end of motor sport for many years, but even before the war had started Mercedes had already invaded France. They sent five of their 4.5litre four-cylinder cars, producing 110bhp, to the French Grand Prix. The race brought heartbreak for French hero Georges Boillot who while leading in his 4.4 litre Peugeot retired on the last lap. This heart-breaking retirement allowed Mercedes to take the first three places. It was to be an uncomfortable omen of thing to come. After the war advances in mechanical development were rapid. The war brought significant improvements in designs and metallurgy. By 1920 many exciting new cars were appearing from manufacturers like Ballot, Peugeot, Sunbeam, and from America, Duesenberg and Miller. Duesenberg entered four of their sleek white and blue cars for the 1921 French Grand Prix held at Le Mans.

To the shock of the European manufactures, after a tremendous dual with a Ballot driven by another

American de Palma, they won the race with Jimmy Murphy driving. These Duesenberg cars were the first to use hydraulic brakes, a system designed by Scots born Malcolm Loughead, who later spelt his name Lockheed. This name is now synonymous with vehicle braking systems.

Racing at Brooklands re-started in 1920. It was still the main outlet for motor sport in England and the most important for vehicle and engine development.

The motor racing was diverse. A handicapping system allowed cars of all sizes and power to compete from little Austin 7's to Aero engine monsters. Record breaking attempts were constant and increasing numbers of specialist magnificent aero machines were built to raise the speeds ever higher. The all-time outright circuit lap record was set by John Cobb driving the magnificent 24 litre NapierRailton at 143.43mph.

Racing at Brooklands finally ended with the outbreak of the Second World War. Too severely damaged in the war made repairs uneconomic when hostilities ended.

In 1923 a race was first held which would become the most famous race in the world, The Le Mans 24 Hours. Winning this race soon became an obsession for motor manufactures and drivers from France, Italy, Germany, England, and America. The British have always had a love affair with Le Mans and in 1924 the Bentley 3litre of Duff and Clement won the race.

Bentley has won the race four more times so far. Each year thousands of British fans make the pilgrimage to Le Mans. The race has helped to make names like Ferrari, Jaguar, Porsche and more recently Audi world famous.

The Isle of Man TT race recognised as the most prestigious and oldest motorcycle race. It has proved to be the most dangerous motorcycle road race in the world.

The obsession for motorcycle manufactures and riders was, from the early years, and still is today, winning a Hermes Statue Silver Trophy in a TT race on the Isle of Man. For more than a week each June bikers from all over the world invade the island. All wanting to experience this unique event.

Two other race circuits feature in the story that follows. Both have also played a major part in the development of motor sport development before the Second World War.

Spa Francorchamps, situated in the Forests of the Ardennes in South-eastern Belgium, has long been considered the most challenging and dangerous track in the world. The unpredictable climate of the area can result in parts of the circuit being dry while unseen around the next 120mph turn the track is soaking wet.

First used in 1922 based on a triangle shape with ultra-fast bends and no margin for error. It has always filled drivers with terror and acute pleasure in equal measure. In 1939 the track was altered with the removal of the Virage de l'Ancienne Douanne corner, to give the racing driver one of the most daunting

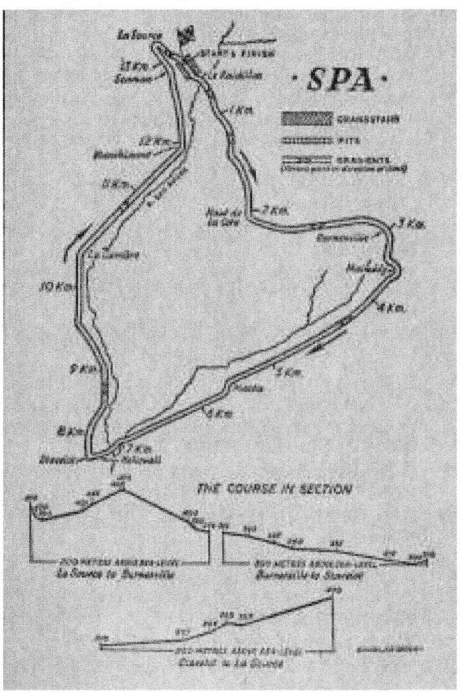

challenges in the world, the addition of Eau Rouge corner.

In 1931 the first purpose-built road circuit in England opened at Donington Park in Derbyshire.
The first car race meeting was held on 25th March 1933, and it soon became a prominent place for racing motorcycles and cars.
Donington Park went on to host the Donington Grand Prix's of the late 1930s which for two years featured the sensational German "Silver Arrows" cars.
Adolf Hitler, reported to have given the German mark equivalent of a twenty-thousand-pound grant to Mercedes to develop a new racing car, "for the honour

of Germany". (This would be the equivalent of over one million UK pounds today). Hitler also invested thousands of marks in Mercedes German rivals Auto Union.

In 1934 the sensational Mercedes W25 raced and won for the first time. Mercedes won four major races and Auto Union three in 1934. For the following five years the Germans dominated Grand Prix racing.

These Silver Arrows "invaded" England twice in 1937 and 1938
Auto Union cars won both races at Donington Park with Bernard Rosemeyer victorious the first year. When Rosemeyer, tragically killed trying to break speed records, Tazio Nuvolari became the star team driver, winning in 1938.

These famous race circuits all play important parts in the following story. Over three generations, and three books, "Deadly Obsessions" charts the fortunes of two families and their addiction to speed , has on their lives.

Dedicated to the memory of all those riders and Drivers' who have paid the ultimate price of their passion for speed.

Chapter One

The clock in the tower of St Mary's church made its ninth strike, and quiet returned to the cramped kitchen of Forge Cottage. The 28th of July 1899 was the hottest day of the year. The heat-soaked clutch walls created oppressive heat in every room.

The heat in the small kitchen compounded by the fire constantly burning in the black iron cooking range set into one wall. A kettle of boiling water steaming on its top.

"Stop swinging your legs." Joan said in a whispered hiss to her young brother Joe whose feet were constantly banging against the old, dark pine, table. Four children sat on mismatched wooden chairs around the table standing in the centre of the kitchen while their father, Charlie Cartland, continued his nonstop pacing. The grating sound from his large hobnail boots as each step hit the stone floor was now the only sound in the room.

With darkness encroaching, Joan, the eldest of the children, rose to light the two oil lamps on the windowsill and then returned to her chair alongside her sister Edith and brothers John and Joe. All eyes turned to the closed door of the next room as Agnes Willes's raised, desperate voice could be clearly heard.

"Push, Push, Push! Please, my dear, just once more," the anxious midwife pleaded to Mary Cartland. It had been eight hours since Mary's labour had started. Mary had been in pain and pushing for hours. Now, she was utterly exhausted,

With a long, piercing cry, signalling a final effort, Mary pushed again, and at last, a bloodied baby boy was born. Then. No sound from the mother or baby.

Mary Cartland had suffered a devastating heart attack.

Agnes gently picked up the child and pressed him between her large, soft breasts. Her sobs began slowly, the tears gently running down her cheeks, but soon she was gulping at air, and the sobs became a wail. A muffled, whine-like noise came from the sticky red mess between her breasts. She glanced down at the baby, who opened one eye and screamed. Agnes looked at the now peaceful face of Mary and then again at the angry, red-faced tiny body she was holding. Tears flowed freely down Agnes' cheeks as she whispered to the dead woman.

"What a terrible waste. I'm afraid this child will soon join you, my dearest girl. I can't imagine this little mite lasting more than a week."

Agnes Willes had delivered babies in Burlham for over 30 years, including Mary's four other children. Mary Cartland had been her only daughter.

Agnes carried the screaming, tiny bundle out of the small bedroom to the rest of his family; all the children stood up as she entered.

"You have another son, Charlie," she nervously said to the giant of a man standing before her.

"Would you like to hold him?"
Pushing past her, Charlie snarled,

"Keep that screaming brat quiet, I want my Mary." Charlie strode into the room and slammed the door. The family in the kitchen heard no noise for twenty seconds. Then, a mighty, almost inhuman howl came from the room.

Agnes rushed the baby out of the house, afraid of what Charlie would do the next time he saw him. The four Cartland children waited nervously in the kitchen for five long minutes, unsure how to react. Suddenly, the door burst open, and their father rushed past them all. Banging the front door behind him, he left the house without saying a word.

Joan led the other children into their mother's room where they tearfully waited, watching her still form until the doctor, summoned by Agnes, arrived to take charge.

Charlie Cartland remained drunk for two days but did manage to sober up on the third day for his wife's burial.

The baby, named Frank by his sister Joan, was a fighter and proved his grandmother wrong. Agnes had found a wet nurse in the next village who was happy to feed the baby and keep him safe from his father. With help from his eldest sister Joan, Agnes cared for Frank in her old cottage for the first 12 months of his life.

After Frank's first birthday, Agnes returned him to his home, where he continued to thrive. He grew into a healthy boy, raised by sisters Joan and Edith. During those early years, Frank was ignored by his father, Charlie, and by his two elder brothers, John and Joe.

***

From the beginning of the nineteenth century, the Cartland family had been blacksmiths in Burlham, A small village standing on the chalk marl slope at the edge of the Fens in Cambridgeshire.

At the turn of the twentieth century, village life revolved around the three pubs and the imposing village church of St Mary's.

The church was rebuilt one hundred years earlier after lightning destroyed its tower. St Mary's had stood on the site for over eight hundred years, and it was easy to see why. Constructed on the only high ground in the village, the grand building looked out over the Fens towards Ely Cathedral, ten miles distant.
It also looked down with an aloof air on the village and its Burlham congregation.

Two hundred yards down the lane, past the Red Lion pub, stood the Blacksmith's Forge. The Blacksmith's Forge was a place of contrasts.
During the day, it was hot, bright, and full of sharp, loud noises, with the pungent mixed smells of horse sweat and smoke. When darkness descended, it became a sinister place: silent, grimy, and full of dark shadows, with a hint of movement in corners just out of sight. One small, high window reluctantly allowing in the natural light.

Behind the forge, a cobbled yard led to, four roomed, Forge Cottage. The smell of a hundred years of accumulated smoke permeated its walls and furniture, and the cottage's low ceilings gave it a claustrophobic feel. Frank slept on a small and narrow horsehair bed in the corner of a room shared with his two brothers. His two sisters shared another room, while their father, Charlie, had the smallest room for himself.

Once a week, the family took turns for their weekly wash in an old tin tub placed in front of the kitchen range. Water was drawn from the well in the back garden and heated on the range. A gravel path descended from the well to a brick shed at the bottom of the garden, which housed the earth closet. From the age of seven, when he was big enough to lift the bucket, emptying it when necessary, became Frank's job. Joe had been more than happy to pass on this job to his younger brother.

"I've had the shit job long enough. Now it's your turn," Joe had said with a grin. "It's my birthday present to you." Being the youngest of the five children, Frank accepted the job without protest.

There were good reasons for his compliance. Their father, Charlie, had become sullener and more short-tempered in recent years. He ran the household out of fear, drank heavily and continued to blame Frank for Mary's death. Without the controlling influence of this wife Charlie felt lost and impotent.

Villagers in Burlham knew Charlie Cartland had a violent temper. Nicknamed "Iron Hand," he was Cambridgeshire's most feared fast bowler. That was until Charlie was banned from playing cricket.

The nickname came from Charlie's years spent working the blacksmith forge, where tiny slivers of molten metal would fly off the orange hot iron he would hammer and shape into horseshoes and all forms of farm and household implements.

Slivers would land on Charlie and burn unnoticed into his hand and forearm. Over the years, slivers became permanently embedded in his flesh. At 6 feet tall and weighing 15 stone, Charlie had the strength of an ox. and struck a trembling fear into all the batters who had to face his bowling.

Seeing this black-haired, bearded giant rushing towards them with a hard cricket ball in his hand, the metal implants glinting in the sun, was enough to make even the bravest batsman quake in their boots.

The cricket ban came in September 1906. Burlham were playing in the Cambs Cup final against their bitter rivals, the village of Moreton. It had been a close match, Burlham needing just two wickets for victory. When the team captain gave the ball to Charlie for his final over, success looked almost inevitable. Charlie charged in to deliver the red ball, which thundered hard into the pads of the Moreton batter.

"Howzat!" roared Charlie. Usually, when Charlie appealed for a leg before the wicket (LBW), his roar and intimidating stare ensured that the umpire would raise his finger. But this brave soul said:

"Not out".

"What do you mean? That was fucking out!" screamed Charlie into the poor man's face.

"It was not out," repeated the trembling umpire as beads of sweat formed on his forehead. A quick left hook from Charlie, and the umpire was out with a broken jaw. Charlie never played cricket again.

For the slightest reason, Charlie would take his belt to Frank, usually when he'd come home from the pub drunk. The other children were too afraid to try and stop him.

The latest trigger for violence came on a cold November night. Frank was ten years old. He had forgotten to call after school on the local farmer, Albert Betts. He was meant to pick up the three pounds owed to Charlie for shoeing one of the farmer's Shire horses. It had been late when Frank arrived home.

"Where's the money, Frank?" his worried sister Joan said the moment her brother entered the cottage.

"Father will be home soon, and he'll be expecting it." Frank had been happy until that moment. Now he shivered, his throat dry and fear cramped his belly.

"I ... I was going to pick it up, but I forgot. His voice no more than a whisper. "There's a new steam engine working in the Fens, and I went to see that instead."

By pub closing time, the tension in the cottage was palpable.

"Where's that useless little runt? He was supposed to bring my money to the pub," raged angry and drunk Charlie Cartland as he staggered into the cottage.

He was waving the strap he used on his youngest son in his right hand. Frank could see the strap hanging from the giant iron fist from his hiding place behind his sisters in the corner of the kitchen. It was big, wide, and worn, and Frank knew it hurt like hell.

"Come out from there, you little piece of shit," shouted Charlie when he saw him. He grabbed a handful of Franks hair and dragged him out from behind his sisters' skirts. The other children sat still and remained silent.

Out in the yard, Charlie threw Frank down hard onto the sharp flint cobbles and, giving Frank a firm kick, shouted,

"I wish you had never been fucking born, you should have died, not my Mary."

There was a loud, sharp crack as he brought the strap down hard on Frank's back and thighs. Pain shot through him, as he desperately clung to the thought, *I must keep quiet. I must stay silent.* After all the other beatings he'd suffered, he knew he must not call out.

During the first few beatings, Frank had cried, I'm sorry; I'm sorry, please stop hitting me. But that always enraged Charlie, and he would hit him harder. So now, his face pressed hard into the icy cobbles, Frank lay still, eyes tightly shut, silently biting back the tears and the pain. To help, he escaped into his private dream world.

I am running fast through the field of ripe barley. My bare body is warmed by the hot sun. I'm lost, near the centre of the field, where the tops of the golden yellow stalks are higher than my head. Breathless, I stop and lie down. Swallowed by the barley, I look up into the cloudless, deep blue sky.

Alone and happy, I close my eyes. The buzzing busyness of bees, bugs and flies, swamp my senses. The barley ears whisper to me in the breeze, their fine hairs sway like the wispy strands of an old man's hair.

Suddenly. A sharp pain. Pain like the worst toothache, and Frank's ribs immediately hurt against the hard, cold cobbles once again.

By the time Charlie had tried of the beating, Frank had lost count of the number of times his father had hit him. Frank opened one eye and looked up to see Charlie clutching his stomach. He closed his eyes again, just in time. Charlie retched, and a stream of stinking, steaming sick spewed over Frank's face and hair. With a final hard kick into Frank's ribs, Charlie turned and staggered back to his bedroom.

When Charlie had gone, Joan rushed out. She gently lifted Frank off the cobbles and carried him back into the cottage.

"That's the last time I'll let him do this to me," Frank said quietly as Joan gently cleaned the foul-smelling mess from his hair and face. "I promise you I'll kill him first."

"Don't talk like that, Frank. You know he doesn't mean it; it's just the drink that does it. He didn't drink so much before mother died." Quickly adding.

"But it is not your fault."

Joan held a cold, wet cloth to the large red welts growing on Frank's thin, white thighs and added, "You will just have to try not to upset him so much."

Frank's back, thighs and ribs hurt, but his head was clear. He was sure he would consummate his threat to kill his father one day. Even at ten years old, he knew he would need to be patient and must take more beatings before he was strong enough to fulfil his promise. In the meantime, he would try to keep out of his father's way.

Each Sunday morning, the Cartland family dressed in their best clothes and walked up the hill to St Mary's church. Frank hated Sundays. He always found wearing a shirt, tie, and best short trousers extremely uncomfortable.

The family pew of dark oak was situated in the third row from the back, on the right-hand side of the aisle. The pew was black with age and hard; it felt like he was sitting on a lump of old iron. It was particularly excruciating if the Sunday came soon after a beating from his father.

The old church was forever cold, with icy drafts curling around his bare legs, giving him goose pimples. Compounding his misery the endless droning sermons of the vicar, Reverend Walter Sexton, always made him feel very unhappy.

"If there is a God, why did he let our mother die?" he had asked the vicar after one service.

"It is not our place to question God's actions, young man," replied Walter Sexton, obviously irritated by being spoken to by a ten-year-old boy. "Your mother is in a much better place than here on this earth. She's at God's side."

Before Frank could reply, Joan had pulled him away.

"I don't believe him, and I don't believe in God," Frank said quietly to Joan as they walked back through the churchyard. They went to Forge Cottage past his mother's grave in the Cartland family plot.

On the Sunday after Frank's latest beating, Joan had been surprised to see him kneeling in the pew, with eyes screwed up, silently mouthing a prayer. However, she was fearful that she knew what he was praying for.

In fact, Frank didn't have to carry out the promise he had made to Joan. Just one month after that last heavy beating, at 6am on a freezing Monday morning in December, Frank made his way across the moonlit, frost capped cobbles of the icy yard.

His morning duty was to light the fire pit in the forge. He had to ensure a good fire when Charlie was ready to start work. He knew a fresh beating would be almost inevitable if the fire was not hot enough.

Straining to push open the heavy oak door, the smell hit Frank. Mixed with the expected smoky, horsey stench of the forge he was expecting was the distinctive smell of their outhouse - the smell of shit and piss. In the dim, early morning light shining through the small forge window, he could just make out, hanging from the massive black beam that ran the length of the forge, the body of his father.

Frank's first reaction was to turn and run, but instead, he moved slowly towards the gently swaying body hanging next to the massive forge anvil. Curious, he stood still and looked up at the staring eyes of the vast shell that had been his father. Not with any sadness, just a growing sense of relief. Charlie Cartland a man of few words and even fewer smiles, had until now cast a long dark shadow over Frank's life.

A shout of.

"Frank!" causes him to turn. A black silhouette in the forge doorway was that of his sister, Joan.

"Get away from there!" she screamed. Rushing in, she grabbed Frank's arm and dragged him back to the cottage. Seeing his distressed sister and brother as they burst into the house, John ran to the forge.

He soon returned to the shocked family, who were huddled around the kitchen range, their faces reflecting the suddenness of the tragedy.

"Looks like the old man is dead," John said bluntly, "Joe, run off and fetch Constable Clarke."

"Then cycle over to get Doctor Jones," added Joan.

Joe set off, and the others waited; no words were spoken. Twenty minutes later, Joe returned with Constable Tom Clarke.

Constable Clarke and John went into the forge. Together, they managed to cut Charlie down.

Later that morning, Doctor Jones arrived. After ten minutes with Charlie, he walked into the cottage. He announced to the children, all sitting around the kitchen table.

"I'm sorry to have to confirm that your father has died. He appears to have hanged himself."

Doctor Jones wasn't surprised that there were no tears. His news was met by a heavy silence from the five children.

Charlie Cartland was buried next to his beloved wife Mary in the churchyard of St Mary's, up the hill from the forge.

The funeral was a small, quiet affair. The children, a collection of Charlie's drinking and old cricketing mates, attended. In total, ten people huddled around the grave. They stood in cold, driving sleet as the Reverend Sexton muttered the few standard words:

"We now commit his body to the ground. Earth to earth ..." At that moment, with the sharp sound of dry dirt crumbling as it hit the wooden lid of his father's coffin, Frank smiled, with the sudden realisation that his nightmare was over.

Ambling back down the path from the churchyard, the small party remained silent. Deep in their own thoughts, heads down against the icy wind as the sleet turned to wet snow.

***

Christmas 1909 should have been the happiest the Cartland children had experienced since their mother died. Two days before the big day, Joan and Edith were making plum Christmas pudding; their mood in the cottage relaxed and happy. For once, the air smelled sweet as the tang of oranges and brandy invaded the room.

Joe and Frank were helping the girls.

"Stop eating the candied peel and nuts, you two," scolded Joan. Then, turning to Frank, she said:

"Make yourself useful. Run to the butchers and pick up the turkey we ordered."

Just as Frank was about to leave, John arrived at the cottage. He was followed by a serious-looking Constable, Tom Clarke and two other police officers.

"I'm sorry, Joan, but we need to ask you all some questions about Charlie," said Tom Clarke. "This is Inspector Davies from Cambridge Police Headquarters." Inspector Davies stepped forward. He was a small, nervous-looking man with a pencil-black moustache and straight, slicked-back black hair.

"Do any of you know what your father's movements were on the night before he died?" he said bluntly in a surprisingly deep voice. He directed his question at Joan.

"As far as we know, he went to the pub as usual, and then I heard him come in around eleven o'clock," she answered.

"Why are you asking? You know he killed himself."

"Yes, of course, we know that", Inspector Davies replied with a sharp, superior air. "But we have found a body, and it's someone your father used to visit".

"Whose body is it?" said Joan; her voice had also become sharp and high-pitched. She didn't like the tone of this horrid little man. The other four children remained silent.

"I can't tell you that, just that it's a woman's body, and it's someone known to have given sexual favours to your father."

There followed a full minute of shocked silence. John looked very pale and shook slightly as he spoke for the first time.

"Where'd you find her?" he asked quietly. Turning to look up at him, Inspector Davies said, after a long pause.

"My, my, you're a big fellow. You must be John. Constable Clarke has told me about you."

Tom Clarke looked nervous as John gave him a long, hard stare.

"As I told your sister, I can't tell you any more at present, but the victim did put up a hell of a struggle. That's why we need to dig up your father's body to see if it shows any signs of a fight."

"No," screamed Joan as she leapt up and beat her fists into the chest of the inspector, almost knocking the surprised little man over. "Leave him in peace; he was always getting into fights; it doesn't mean he killed anyone."

John and Edith gently pulled Joan away and eased her onto a chair at the kitchen table. Flustered, the inspector said sharply,

"You can get into trouble attacking a police officer, but I will overlook it this time."

Without another word, he turned and walked out of the cottage. After the police had gone, Frank asked Joe:

"What are sexual favours?"

"You will find out soon enough when you're older," was all Joe would say.

Frank was confused. He knew John had also been out that night. He had heard his brother arrive home around the same time as their father. *Why didn't John tell the inspector this?*

Sleeping for all the children was difficult after this revelation. Frank lay in his narrow bed, staring into the blackness and listening to the sobs of his sisters in the next room. At sunrise on Christmas Eve, despite his family's continued protests, police dug up the coffin of Charlie Cartland. They sent his body to Addenbrooks Hospital in Cambridge for a post-mortem.

"The police won't find anything. Our dad couldn't have killed anybody," said Joan to no one in particular. She, Joe, Edith, and Frank sat around the kitchen table at first light, their faces reflecting a mix of fear and uncertainty.

John wasn't at home. He had gone out to the pub the previous day, soon after the police left. By closing time, he had passed out on the floor of the Red Lion. Leaving him there, the landlord locked the doors and went to bed. Staggering back in the early hours, John went straight into the forge. Edith sat quietly sobbing as she always did when upset. Joe and Frank were silent and sullen as they listened to the dull, constant hammering from the forge. With a big sigh, Frank said,

"We will never be free of our old man. Even when he's dead, he still brings us misery."
No one answered him.

On a cold but dry Christmas morning, the Cartland family, united in silence, made their way to St Mary's church for the 10 a.m. Christmas service. As they walked, their heads held high, a silent show of their unity. For once, Frank was content to put on his best Sunday clothes.

Not a word about the police visit had been spoken within the family. The previous night, the local gravedigger, Walter Williams, had, for the price of a pint, let the locals at the Red Lion know that he had spent the early hours of that morning digging up Charlie Cartland's coffin. The news and speculation had spread around the village like wildfire, intensifying the gossip and speculation.

Unsurprisingly, the church congregation stopped murmuring and gossiping as the Cartland family, dressed in their best Sunday clothes, filed into their usual black pew, the wooden bench creaking loudly as they sat down.

Revered Sexton had made the theme of his sermon Sins of the Flesh. Frank did not understand his words, so as usual, his unhappy mind went to a better place.

It is early on a warm spring day. A ground mist rises slowly from the ditch like a wet grass fire. I'm sitting on the bank at the top of the Devil's Ditch, watching the rising mist and the rabbits hopping. Hundreds of the little furry brown bundles are digging out the holes in their burrows. As they busily continue their excavations, their efforts leave a white chalk tear on the green slope. Chalkhill Blue butterflies have settled on the grass stems next to me, opening their wings to catch the warming morning sun.

What's that? I can see something glinting in the weak sun at the bottom of the ditch; I'm sliding down the bank to investigate. There's a golden, jewelled dagger amongst the excavated white chalk rubble. I'm bending down to pick it up.

Joe dug his elbow into Frank's ribs, and the dagger disappeared.

"Come on; wake up, Frank," he whispered. "The service has finished." Filing out of the church, their friends in the congregation avoided the Cartlands, and none seamed prepared to speak to them. Not even to wish them a happy Christmas.

"It's like they think they might catch something horrible from us," said a sobbing Joan as the sad group ambled home

John usually spent his days alone. Now, even on Christmas Day, he immediately stripped off his suit after church, put on his overalls and went straight to the forge. The other children could hear the sharp sound of his heavy hammer striking the anvil and the sudden hiss from the red-hot metal as he plunged a new horseshoe into the water trough.

Throughout the long afternoon, Joan, Edith, Joe, and Frank sat quietly around the old pine table. Their Christmas dinner cold and barely touched in front of them. No one was in the mood for food or any of the usual party games, which Frank had always looked forward to in previous years.

By 4 pm, darkness crept across the room like a black, grasping shadow. Joe got up and walked slowly through each room of the silent cottage, lighting the oil lamps to banish the cold, dark night from their home

The Cartland family's distress had been triggered by Billy Webb and Eric Folds' upsetting discovery in the river at Farwell. Both boys were ten years old and lived in the village. Billy's dad was the local milkman, so Billy was always up early. Two days before Christmas, he went around Eric's house and threw small stones onto his window to wake him up.

The boys arrived at the Lode in Farewell early, around 6.30 am, their hearts brimming with excitement for their secret pike fishing expedition. This was a tradition passed down through generations of Farewell boys.

The pike in the river at Farewell Lode could grow to more than thirty pounds, a fact that fuelled the boys' excitement. It was the sole ambition of many of the young lads in the area to catch one of these monstrous fish. Billy, using live bait, a small roach he had caught earlier, was particularly eager to make a catch.

They had been casting for half an hour without success when he felt a tug on his line and made a hard strike. In an excited voice, he shouted across to Eric,

"Get the gaff ready, Eric, I've got a bloody whopper here."

He pulled hard, his fishing rod bending almost double and in danger of breaking.

Billy, straining to hold the fishing rod, grunted, "Come on, help me with it, I've never felt anything as big as this before". They were expecting a long, hard struggle to land a giant pike.

Together, they slowly reeled in Billy's catch, surprised and disappointed that it was not putting up much of a fight. Grunting, both boys pulled together.

"Here it comes," shouted Eric as a light shape appeared towards the surface.

The first thing they saw was a small foot. Then, a leg up to the thigh rose out of the water like a surfacing submarine. They could clearly see Billy's three-barbed hook embedded deep into the stark white flesh. The roach remains were still on the hook and appeared to be nibbling at the leg.

"Oh, bloody hell." Squealed Billy.

The boy's nerves went on at that moment. They dropped the fishing rod and ran to the closest building, the Anglers Arms Pub. Crying and distressed, they hammered on the door until the owner, Archie Law, finally opened it.

"What the hell..." Archie exclaimed, angry at being disturbed so early.

"There ... there's a body in the water," stammered Billy.

" Billy caught it" exclaimed Eric trying to distance himself from the trauma. Both boys were by now hysterical.

After they had managed to blurt out their tale, Archie left them with his wife and hurried to the police house. He and the constable returned to the riverbank, found Billy's fishing rod in the water, and, with difficulty, pulled the body to the riverbank.

Later that morning, the doctor, Howard Jones, arrived. He quickly examined the body and announced that he thought it had been in the water for at least two weeks. News soon spread around the village of the gruesome discovery, and a small crowd of locals turned up to have a look. With only one village constable to control them, they quickly gathered around the body.

"Oh my God, it's Maggie Munford," shouted someone in the crowd. When he occasionally travelled to The Kings Head pub in Farewell, Maggie was often Charlie Cartland's drinking partner.

Everyone knew she offered sexual favours in exchange for drinks or money and that Charlie was one of her customers.

The investigation of the exhumed body of Charlie was inconclusive. There were no apparent signs of a struggle. His coffin was reburied the following day without a further ceremony. With no other suspects for the murder, the police quickly decided that Charlie Cartland must have been responsible and had hanged himself in a fit of remorse.

"It's so convenient for them, isn't it? He's not here to speak for himself," Frank overheard Joan's frustrated whisper to John in the next room. John, as usual, remained silent. The Cartland family all aware of the villagers' belief that Charlie was the one who had murdered Maggie.

The local, then the national press arrived in the village wanting information about the Cartland family. For a supply of beers in the Red Lion, Charlie's old mates were happy to tell them what a drunk he had been and how violent he could be. Charlie Cartland was immediately depicted in the press as a monster. With the police not inclined to pursue any more inquiries, it became a simple case. Charlie Cartland, in a fit of rage, had murdered his lover, Maggie Munford.

The Cartland family found themselves increasingly isolated and ignored. Frank's old friends now hurled insults at him: 'killer's boy,' 'bad blood Cartland,' and worse, in the days between Boxing Day and New Year's Day.

The reporters had effectively trapped the family in their cottage, cutting them off from the outside world. Every time they ventured outside, they were bombarded by questions from the crowd of news reporters. By New Year's Eve the press had become bored, and with no further sensationalist headlines to create, finally left the family alone.

Then, on the morning of New Year's Day, 1910, another body was found. Frank believed he was the first from his family to hear about it.

To get away from the melancholy atmosphere in the cottage on New Year's morning, he had gone for a long walk up to and along the Devil's Dyke. Frank always found that this was the best place to escape the harsh reality of the real world. He was usually optimistic, but that day, he felt depressed about the future.

At just ten years old, Frank found it difficult to comprehend all the tragic events that had unfolded in his short life. It was hard to cope with. Frank never knew his mother, had a father who hated him and beat him regularly, and one who now everyone thought of as a murderer.

Wandering along the path through the gorse bushes and crimson-headed thistles on top of the dyke, he saw a huddle of people gathered around something in the ditch, about two hundred yards from the road that connected Burlham to Farwell.

Frank slid down the bank towards the group to get a better look. As he moved closer, he noticed one person he recognised. It was the that horrible small, plain-clothed police inspector, who had called at the Forge Cottage on Christmas Eve asking about Charlie. Inspector Davies noticed Frank coming down the slope and turned towards him.

"Hold on, Sonny, you can't come any closer," he said.

Frank quickly turned left and ran back up the steep bank of the dyke.

"Hey, come down from there," shouted the Inspector. But Frank was too fast, and upon reaching the bank's top, he peered down onto the scene below. There, lying in the long, rough grass and nettles, Frank could see a chalky white, naked body. Although it was lying face down, he decided it must be a girl because of her lengthy, black hair.

"Get out of here, now!" shouted the panting Inspector as he struggled up the slope.

Frank did get out and ran the mile back to the cottage without stopping. He burst in as Joan and Edith were having a cup of tea.

"What on earth's the matter now?" asked a startled Joan.

"They've found another body up at Devil's Dyke," blurted a breathless Frank.

"Who is it this time?" Joan said slowly. Frank explained what he had seen and how the Inspector had chased him away.

"Quickly go into the forge and tell John what has happened," said Joan.

"Can't you tell him?" asked Frank nervously. Over the previous few days, he had become terrified of John, who had started to look at him like his father used to. Joan came back from the forge looking puzzled.

"What's the matter?" said Frank.

"When I told him what you'd seen, he just dropped his hammer and walked out," she said. Once more, they sat around the kitchen table, lost in their thoughts. It was almost dark when John arrived home. He had obviously had a heavy drinking session; they could smell the beer on him. But to their surprise, he started talking - a rare event.

"That inspector and two other coppers came into the pub," he said in a slightly slurred voice. "One copper said they found the body of a woman and that she'd been murdered, recently like, strangled - same as that other old slag - so our old man didn't do it."

John swayed into his bedroom, the room he had taken when their father died, and slammed the door. The other children looked at each other with a nervous smile, not sure if it was a relief regarding the news or for hearing John say so much. Frank had never heard him string more than three or four words together before.

Over the following days, the dark cloud hanging over the Cartland family gradually lightened as news went around about the new murder.

Frank smiled when his friends said they hadn't really believed his old man had done it. Never one to bear grudges, Frank accepted the return of his mates' friendship.

The police quickly discovered that the latest body was that of another well-known prostitute, Annie Hunt, from the nearby village of Morden. She worked part-time as a barmaid in the Prince Regent pub in Morden but was better known for her late-night work. She had been working at the pub two nights previously. This time, the police had to look much harder for evidence. They certainly couldn't blame the ghost of Charlie Cartland for this murder.

Two days later, their Uncle Charlie rushed into the forge cottage.

"The police have arrested someone for the murders," he said. "I've just been in Newmarket and seen coppers leading him out of Merrywell Stables." "Who is it? asked Frank excitedly.

"It's one of their stable lads, Ralph Stock. People say he has been acting strangely lately. The lads said someone had reported to the police that they saw him with Annie Hunt when she disappeared".

"That doesn't mean he's guilty," said Joan, breaking into sobs, "they said father had been seen with that other girl on the night she was killed. I'll just be glad when this is all over."

The surly Ralph Stock had never been popular in Newmarket. He was a bitter and difficult failed jockey whose wife had left him for another, more successful jockey. Now, he spent his meagre wages on gambling and drinking. Ralph Stock, questioned at Cambridge police station unremittingly for two full days, suddenly broke down and confessed to both murders.

The Cambridge Evening News reported that he had admitted he had lost his temper with the women and strangled them when they had made fun of his height and bandy legs. Police didn't question how a five-foot, eight stone man had managed to move the bodies and dump them. One in the river and the other at the Devil's Dyke.

Ralph Stock was committed to Bedford Jail, with his trial date set for October. Although at the trial, he denied ever admitting to the murders, the prosecution produced two fellow stable workers and Ralph's ex-wife as witnesses. The ex was happy to give evidence against him, stating that he often beat her up when drunk and had once tried to strangle her. The stable workers, two men Stock had crossed in the past, were willing to swear that they had seen him with Annie Hunt only an hour before she disappeared.

Although this was the only tangible evidence the prosecution had produced, it was enough to sway the jury.

It took two hours of deliberation before Ralph Stock, despite the scant evidence, was declared guilty by a unanimous majority.

Ralph Stock was hanged in Bedford jail on November 1st, 1911, bringing both murder cases to a close.

The press had soon lost interest in the story just two weeks after Ralph Stock's arrest, and they moved on to more exciting news in London. In Houndsditch, there had been several shootings, and three policemen had been killed. This soon made the events in Burlham of little national interest.

"Thank goodness that's all over, and we can get back to our normal lives," said Joan as she put on her best coat and hat and went up to the church to give thanks.

The villagers of Burlham settled back into their everyday lives and quiet routines. The Cartland family, with a palpable sense of relief, also went back to normal. Some of their neighbours even apologised for the way they had treated them.

January 1911 was exceptionally cold, with sharp frosts and heavy snowfall. A blanket of pure, bright white snow fell over the whole village, endeavouring to wipe away the terrible events of the past December.

Chapter two

While Frank Cartland grew from child to young man in an overcrowded cottage in a small Cambridgeshire village, George William Marshall also grew up in a small village. But the similarity ended there.

George was raised in the Marshall family's imposing Elizabethan Manor House, which stood at the top of the Sussex village of Sefton.

Sefton Manor, a sprawling 300-year-old, 30 roomed house, was a testament to the Marshall family's wealth and status. Nestled in 200 acres of picturesque rolling pastureland on the slopes of the South Downs, it was an imposing sight.

The Lord of the Manor owned most of the tithe cottages in the village, with many of their tenants being employed on the estate. George, a member of this illustrious family, lived in the Manor with his parents, Lord John William Marshall and Lady Victoria Marshall, and his twin elder brothers, Matthew, and Stuart. The family's status was further accentuated by the employment of 20 additional domestic servants.

Born on the 21st of May 1901, five years after his brothers, George was a lonely child. His father had been MP for Chichester and was now in the House of Lords, as his father and grandfather had been before him.

George saw little of his parents. Lord Marshall spent most of his time away from Sefton Manor at the family townhouse in Mayfair. His mother Victoria showed little interest in the young George, leaving his upbringing to his nanny and their many servants. All her attention was directed toward his spoilt and selfish elder twin brothers, who were the future of the Marshall dynasty.

Victoria Marshall's also grew up in a wealthy old southern English family before marrying John Marshall in 1895. Her family roots went back to Elizabethan times. More impressive than that, the Marshalls could trace their ancestry back almost eight hundred years to the crusader William Marshall, 1st Earl of Pembroke. His yellow and green halved coat of arms, with its red dragon rampant, was proudly displayed throughout the Manor.

It was tradition that close to their tenth birthday, the sons of each generation of Marshalls would be taken to the Templar Chapel in London. There, they would leave a drop of their own blood and place a kiss on the imposing cold effigy covering the stone coffin of their ancient ancestor, William Marshall.

George's formative years were extremely easy, thanks to his full-time nanny, his governess, and plenty of servants. He didn't have to think or do much for himself. By nine, he had grown into a slightly chubby boy with the 'Marshall look'.

Neither Victoria nor John Marshall were handsome, and unfortunately, they passed these genes onto their boys. All three were thickset and round-faced, with high foreheads and flat chins. They had blond, straight hair, slightly heavy eyebrows, and small grey/green eyes.

Fortunately, the boys all grew to around five feet nine inches tall, which helped negate their less attractive features.

George's spoilt upbringing had made him quite lazy. He was also a solitary boy with no one his age to play with. His one constant companion was his Steiff teddy bear, which he had been given on his second birthday. George secretly named the bear Bertie after his father's brother.

Uncle Bertie was the one person who showed any interest in George.

The bear had coarse hair the colour of dark honey, long arms, and brown, glass eyes. A broad, stitched black line made up its mouth, which was turned down at the corners, giving it a mournful look. From that second birthday onwards, George and Bertie were inseparable.

Two days after his tenth birthday George found himself packed off to boarding school. On the way to the school, Lady Victoria took George to London for the ceremony with his ancient ancestor. As he reluctantly entered the cold, damp and silent chapel, George whispered,

"Do I really have to kiss him, Mother?"

"Of course, you do, silly boy. It's your duty as a Marshall," his mother said as she pushed him towards the imposing coffin. Reluctantly shuffling across the grey flagstones, George climbed onto the box placed against the coffin. He leant over the stone beard and kissed the cold, stone, dry lips to do his duty. Quickly, his mother pricked George's right thumb with a needle.

"Ouch," cried George as she squeezed his thumb hard, forcing a sizeable red drop of Marshall blood onto the grey praying hands of the effigy of his ancient ancestor.

His duty done, Victoria, without a kiss or any sign of affection, led George out of the dark chapel and into the fresh spring air. Waiting outside the chapel was James Bird, the Marshall chauffeur. He stood with the back door of the family Rolls-Royce open.

"Get in, George, I expect I will see you at half term," said his mother.

Then, without another word, Victoria turned and walked towards the Embankment.

The ruby-red Rolls-Royce Silver Ghost, with a limousine body and tulip back, was registered as number M46. It was James' pride and joy. With George sitting alone on the vast, leather back seat of the Rolls, quietly sucking his sore thumb, James drove straight to Leamington Hall boarding school. As George gave Bertie, tucked safely inside his jacket, a comforting squeeze, a single tear ran slowly down his cheek.

George was almost asleep as the Rolls purred along the school's long, winding drive. The sudden crunching of tyres on gravel brought George fully awake. With apprehension, he looked out at the imposing, red bricked building as the Rolls glided to a stop.

"Enjoy yourself, Master George," said James as he opened the Rolls door for him. "I'll be back for you at half term."

Having removed cases from the boot, James drove off, leaving George and his two small leather suitcases in front of the large, dark brown, oak front door of Leamington Hall. The door had a large black knocker shaped like a lion's head, but George couldn't reach it. The door swung open as he stood looking up at the lion and wondering what to do. A short, round lady with smiley eyes greeted him.

"Welcome to your new home, George," she said. "We have been expecting you. I am Matron Greaves. I will be here to look after you if you have any illness or worries. While you are at Leamington, I will take over the role of your mother.

George looked up into this friendly, wrinkled face and thought, *I really hope you will not be like my mother.*

At first, boarding school was a real shock for George. All the boys were woken up at 6 a.m. every day, and he shared a room with seven other boys. This was a complete contrast to his old life, and adjustment was difficult. But, for the first time in his life, he had friends.

At Leamington School, he found that most other boys also felt dumped and abandoned by their families. That first night, as he lay silently in his small bed cuddling Bertie tightly, he heard sobbing.

"Why are you crying?" he whispered to Simon, the little boy in the bed next to him in their dormitory, "I miss my mummy and my little sister," said Simon in a small, squeaky voice. George was suddenly surprised to realise that he didn't miss anybody.

"Don't worry, Simon, I'll look after you," he said. Over the following three years, the lonely boys' mutual unhappiness bound them together as they grew into privileged young men.

By his second term, George had settled quite well into the school routines and grown in confidence. With nothing to do back at the manor during the Easter holidays, he walked into the stables where James changed the engine oil on the Rolls. An old magazine lying on the bonnet caught his attention. It had a picture of a car on the cover.

"What's this about?" he asked James as he picked up the magazine.

"It's *Autocar*, a motoring magazine, Master George. It tells you everything about cars and racing," replied James. Excitedly turning the pages, George said,

"Look, it's got pictures of Brooklands in it! My brothers have been there, and I really want to go. Can I borrow this, please, James?"

"Of course, Master George, you can keep it." On his return to Leamington School, George asked James to send copies of *Autocar* whenever he could. He would spend hours reading and re-reading articles on Brooklands and all the fantastic European races.

Unfortunately, to the detriment of his education, George found *Autocar* much more exciting reading than trying to understand Latin verbs.

"What is it that you're always reading?" asked Robin McAlpine, one of the boys in George's dormitory. "It's *Autocar*. It tells me all that is going on in the motor racing world," replied George confidently.

"I know what's going on there. My father had a car built and has raced it at Brooklands," said Robin with a dismissive air.

"Really?" George said excitedly. "I'm going to be a racing motorist when I'm older."

"I am too," said Robin, "and I bet I'll be faster than you."

George, whose confidence suddenly deflated, didn't argue with Robin, but in his dreams, he was always behind the wheel of a racing car, roaring around the Brooklands track and winning races.

Lord John Marshall was a member of the same London Club as Mr. Locke-King, who, in 1907, built the Brooklands race circuit on his Weybridge estate, much to the dismay of his neighbours. John Marshall was a heavy gambler, and as bookmakers were allowed at the track, he was keen to attend this new, exciting form of gambling.

George was almost eleven when he was taken to Brooklands for the first time, and the memories formed that day remained vivid his whole life.

The morning of Sunday, 5th May 1911, was the most important in his young life; he had been looking forward to it for weeks.

It was warm but overcast when James brought the Rolls to the front door of Sefton Manor, and George, dressed in his Sunday best jacket, shirt, and tie, climbed in. His father and brothers also travelled with him, but Victoria Marshall remained home.

"I've been there once and can't imagine why anyone would want to watch those smoky, noisy things," she'd said at breakfast that morning. "There are enough of them rushing around our roads here in Sussex scaring all my horses."

They travelled in silence. George, his nose pressed to the window, watched the dappled greens of the countryside drift by.

The twins had been to Brooklands before, but like their father, they preferred horses to cars, so they had no genuine enthusiasm for the trip. Lord John soon fell asleep, his loud snoring drowning out the quiet purring from the Rolls Royce engine.

Arriving at Brooklands through the tunnel under the track and into the paddock transported George to a new, magical world. Here he had his first sight of the monster racing cars he had only seen in the Autocar magazine.

His first glimpse was of a big, blue car as it powered into sight on the massive, white concrete bowl It was a life-changing experience for any young boy, overpowering their senses with the uniquely rich and pungent smells of burning Castor oil and hot rubber. Incredibly impactful was the ear-hurting, flame-splitting noise coming from the unsilenced engines.

Standing in the dusty, hot paddock, filled with the deafening roar of engines and the acrid smell of burning rubber, George was captivated by the flames and smoke spitting from the open exhaust pipes of Charles Jarrott's 4.5-litre Humber. George shivered as he felt the raw power and excitement of the racing world, which had completely bewitched him.

With his brothers, George watched A.J. Hancock, in his silver 16hp Vauxhall, beat the half-mile record at 97.67mph. The air was thick with the smell of burning fuel, and the ground shook with the thunderous roar of the engines.

"I am going to be a racing motorist when I'm older and drive a car just like this one," declared George, with determination to his brothers. They both laughed.

"You will never be brave enough to do that, Georgie Porgie," said Matthew.

"You even get scared riding your little pony," added Stuart.

It was true. George never felt like he was in control riding his horse, but this was completely different. A racing car had pedals, levers, and a great big steering wheel to control it - it wasn't just some animal with a mind of its own and thin, leather reins to pull on. *I'll show you two*, he thought. *Driving a racing car is what I'm going to do.*

That day, he joined many other young boys in the hero worship of these daring, larger-than-life Brooklands drivers.

Without speaking to his family, George plucked up the courage to convince his chauffeur, James, to teach him to drive. He persistently badgered James for months until he relented. His opportunity arose on a summer's day when his mother was in London, and his father and brothers were at the Goodwood horse races.

Propped up on two cushions, his first attempts caused the Rolls to kangaroo-hop along the drive. However, within an hour, he had mastered the basic controls and was full of confidence. Despite James trying to slow him down, he started causing mayhem at the manor, spraying gravel all over the gardeners and churning up the lawns.

"I want to spend my whole life driving fast cars," said George to anyone who would listen to him.

A week later, while George was in the middle of one of his "laps" of the grounds, his father arrived home. Noticing his young son peering over the steering wheel of the Rolls, he became red with rage. When George noticed his father, he pressed the brake pedal hard, and the Rolls slithered to a stop, leaving two large muddy ruts in the grass.

"What the bloody hell is going on?" Lord Marshall bellowed, his face turning red with rage. "James, I hold you responsible for this madness. Pack your bags now. You are sacked."

George's heart sank with the weight of his father's anger hanging in the air, realizing the consequences of his actions He jumped out of the Rolls and ran up to his father.

"It's all my fault, Father," he said bravely, his voice steady despite the fear in his heart. "I…I made

James teach me to drive. Please don't make him leave; he's the best chauffeur we've ever had."

In fact, James had been the only chauffeur at the manor during George's short life. His father looked down at his youngest son with some surprise. It was the first time George had ever answered him back. After a long pause, he said:

"Very well, he can stay, but you are banned from driving the Rolls. If I hear that you have been driving it again, it will be the worst for you and the sack for him." Lord Marshall turned abruptly and went into the house. George's bravery earned James' respect.

"Thank you for your support, Master George," he said.

A few days later, James was driving George back to Leamington School when he said:

"In one of the stables, Master George is an old three-wheel cyclecar. It's been unused for years, but I'll get the engine running so that when you come back at the end of term, it will be ready for you to use. But not anywhere near your father."

"Thank you, James," replied George, his voice filled with shock and delight. It was the first time in his life that anyone had offered to do something nice for him.

Chapter Three

Although only seventeen, John was already six feet tall and weighed more than thirteen stone. He had become a competent blacksmith, having watched his father since he was a boy. His work was in great demand, and John skilfully continued the family business. With constant physical effort, he grew exceptionally strong.

Disturbingly for Frank, he also looked and started acting increasingly sullen, just like their father.

I am going to have to be careful around him in the future, thought Frank

In looks and nature, Joe and Frank had taken after their mother's side of the family, many of whom were employed around Newmarket, a renowned hub of the horse racing industry. Both boys had black, curly hair and were much smaller and slimmer than John; both had cheeky grins and optimistic natures. Their uncle Charlie was a successful jockey based in Newmarket, a place known for its prestigious races and top-notch trainers. Although he never won any of the noticeably big races, he had a sympathetic way with young racehorses that the trainers loved.

"The trainers all say I've got soft hands," he would jest with Joe and Frank, saying "but what do you two think", after he had playfully given them a hard cuff around the ears. Joe and Frank, both idolized him, seeing in him the father they should've had.

Often, on Sundays, their uncle would visit to have tea with the family. He would turn up driving a small cart pulled by a large goat, a peculiar sight that never failed to amuse the boys. The cart, painted in bright colours, its wheels were adorned with ribbons and bells.

The boys were delighted when Charlie took them for rides around the village in this strange contraption, and they proudly waved to all their friends.

Joe was now fourteen and had left school. All he had ever wanted to do was follow his hero Uncle Charlie and work with horses. On a warm April morning he excitedly came into the cottage.

"Uncle Charlie has found a job for me in Newmarket," he said, his voice filled with excitement. "I'm going to be a famous jockey." His words were greeted with a mix of pride and concern from his family, who knew the challenges that lay ahead for him. With his connections in horse racing, Charlie Willes had arranged a job for Joe as a stable lad in The Meddler Stud.

"You are going to have to work very hard in the stables mucking out and cleaning tack before they let you even ride a horse," said Joan.

Joan, like her brother John, had inherited their father's pessimistic view of life. Unlike Joe and Frank, who loved the thrill and excitement of horse racing.

Frank loved his bigger brother Joe.

"I'm really going to miss you," he whispered as he watched Joe packing his canvas bag ready to leave. Joe always had a certain swagger and an air of confidence that Frank admired. He wanted to be just like Joe when he grew up, and the thought of Joe being moving away caused Frank a pang of loneliness.

"Frankie, my boy, you'll be fine. I'll never be far away from you, remember, just don't go doing anything to upset big John"

In fact, Frank continued seeing Joe often, as Joe would turn up at home once or twice a month, cycling the three miles on an old bike his uncle had given him. He always brought his washing home for his sisters to sort out. Frank looked forward to hearing Joe's wild tales of his adventures in the rough pubs of Newmarket, where he would often find himself after a long day at the stables, rubbing shoulders with jockeys, trainers, and other colourful characters.

At least a few of his tall tales must be true; Frank thought when Joe arrived home one Sunday with a black eye and two missing teeth.

The following two years were uneventful for Frank, if not for the other members of his family. His sisters were both courting local men. Norman Crowe had known Joan since childhood. Their mothers had been best friends and there never seemed any doubt that they would become a couple one day. Like all the other Burlham children, Norman had been very afraid of Charlie Cartland

When Charlie died, Norman wasted no time visiting Joan at every opportunity, and they soon became devoted to each other. Norman was a tall, thin, shy young man. His gentle, easy-going nature meant he was the complete opposite of Joan's father and brother, John.

However, although John's drinking had increased, he was usually sullen and quiet, giving Frank no real trouble.

In March 1913, Edith married her sweetheart, Pat Summers, a stud manager at Snailwell Stud near Newmarket. Ten years older than Edith, Pat was a widower with two young children. His wife had died of scarlet fever in the outbreak of 1908. A cottage was provided with the job, and Edith was happy to have the opportunity to escape from her family home.

"How are you going to manage two young children?" Frank asked earnestly as she packed her case to leave.

"After looking after you and Joe all these years, it's going to be easy," she said, ruffling his hair.

After school and during the holidays, Frank and his mates would rush around all over the village, innocently startling the old folk of Burlham by climbing trees, fishing in the brook, and scrumping apples from the local orchards. Somehow, though, Frank always knew he was slightly different from his schoolmates. For as long as Frank could remember, he felt no fear. The experiences with his father had taught him that he could put up with anything life threw at him.

In the village, standing close to the cricket ground was a massive old Canadian fir tree that had grown to over fifty feet tall. For three generations, many of the more daring local lads tried to climb it but usually lost their nerve, with the bravest getting just over three quarters of the way to the top.

"I dare you to try and climb it, Frank," said Fred Coles in front of the other village boys one hot summer's day.

"If I do, what will you give me?" replied Frank.

"No one's ever climbed it, so we are sure you can't," said Fred. The others nodded in agreement. That challenge was all Frank needed. He was halfway up in a couple of minutes. The gnarled and wide lower branches made it easy. Then it got complicated.

The branches became thin, spiky, and small, sharp twigs dug into his hands and scratched his arms. Frank knew that nothing except a fall would stop him. The boys on the ground below shuffled their feet, kicking the fir cones nervously.

"That's high enough now. Come down now, you'll kill yourself," a worried Fred shouted up to him. Thirty seconds later, swaying on one of the highest branches, Frank shouted down,

"It's great up here, I can see for miles, why don't you all come on up and join meee ..."

The branch that Frank had his arms and legs wrapped around suddenly snapped. The boys all gave out high-pitched screeches as he started to fall. Being in the middle of the tree, his descent was halted by a large branch that stopped him halfway down. Frank was left wedged in its V shape. He hung there, silent, and unmoving, all the wind knocked out of him. His chest was skinned, and his ribs were hurting like hell. Fred, in tears, turned and ran to the forge.

"The ... the branch broke, and Frank is stuck in the big fir tree," he cried to Joan when she opened the door. "Is he hurt?" she whispered, then recovering, she shouted, "John, come quickly, Frank is hurt - and bring the long ladder with you."

John emerged from the forge about a minute later, shouldering the long ladder. He rushed to the cricket ground, with a worried Joan chasing after him. With a determined effort, John reached up and lifted Frank out of the tree. With surprising gentleness, he carried him back to the forge cottage. Joan had already sent Fred off to fetch Doctor Jones. The doctor arrived thirty minutes later.

"He has broken a couple of ribs but should mend alright," said Doctor Jones as he bandaged Frank up. When he left, Joan couldn't contain her frustration, " You are a complete idiot, Frank Cartland. Why did you try a reckless thing like that?"

"Because they all said I couldn't do it," said a grimacing Frank.

He had never felt entirely in step with the boys around him. While they all seemed happy and content with their place in life, he wasn't.

"When I'm grown up, I want to do more with my life than just working on the farms and then drinking in the pub," he would often say to Joan.

"Oh, Frank, you should know your place and be content here. Look how happy your brother Joe is with the horses; you could be like him."

Frank said nothing. He already knew he wasn't going to work for someone else. He would do his own thing, but just now, he had no idea what that was going to be.

Most of the time, Frank didn't dwell on his differences from the other lads, but on odd occasions, he felt that his brain was slightly ahead of his body—not by much, just a split second or two. This gave him sharp wits and the natural ability to make most people like him. It also made him occasionally impulsive and clumsy.

"Why don't you think before you act?" Joan would often ask him after he had broken another cup or plate while helping her with the washing up.

There was one person who didn't seem to like him much: stern old Miss Manners, his schoolteacher. Miss Jane Manners was not actually old. In fact, she was at most forty. But she could have been mistaken for sixty with her greying hair scraped away from her face and swept up into a tight bun, wide hips, ample bosom, and tweed clothes smelling of mothballs. She had always lived with her arthritic mother, and now that she was in her sixties, Jane had to look after her, too. She had been the headmistress of the village school before her daughter. No one seemed to know what had happened to Mr. Manners.

The two ladies lived in their rambling and crumbling old schoolhouse 100 yards from the school door. Frank had never liked going to school; he was always daydreaming and getting into trouble with Miss Manners.

"Your silly boy, Frank Cartland," she would say. "What good will you ever be if you can't even spell simple words? Your brother John was just as stupid."

Spelling and reading had always been difficult for Frank, and he soon lost interest in school, spending most of his time wishing he were somewhere else.

With only two furlongs left in the 2000 Guineas at Newmarket, I urge my horse on, whip in my right hand. The sound of my mount's hooves pounding the ground fills my ears. We're gaining on the leader! The scent of horse sweat, and leather is pungent in the air, and the vibrant purple and gold racing silks are a blur in the sunlight. One final push, and we surge past the leader just as the winning post flashes by. The crowd erupts in a frenzy of excitement. I've won the race by a nose, riding the King's horse.

"Frank CARTLAND, I am talking to you!" Miss Manners and her spelling class brought him back to reality.

Frank, tired of constant trouble, mixed-up letters, and Miss Jane Manners' insults, made a bold decision during Easter break. At just 13, he walked out of his classroom, determined never to return. Frank knew he wasn't stupid; in fact, he believed he was sharper and brighter than most of his classmates. Frustrated, he yearned to move forward with his life.

"What will you do if you don't return to school?" Joan had protested when he had told her he was not going back. Frank suddenly knew. Nearly every grown-up in Burlham now had a bicycle.

"I'm going to repair bikes," was his sudden, confident reply.

When Miss Manners called out Frank's name for the register on the first day back after the Easter break, there was no reply.

"Where is Frank Cartland?" she said sharply to Fred Coles, whom she knew to be one of Frank's friends.

"He's not coming back, Miss," said Fred.

"Well, we will see about that," said Miss Manners indignantly.

After school that first day, Jane Manners went to the Forge Cottage to protest to Joan about Frank's absence. The moment Joan opened the door, Miss Manners said,

"That little brother of yours will be trouble, mark my words. He needs to be back at school where I can watch him." Joan looked down at the angry little round woman in front of her and said slowly,

"I'm sure Frank will be simply fine. You should be pleased at least he won't be any more trouble for you. You can pick on someone else for a change. Now go away."

Before the red-faced teacher could protest, Joan had shut the door in her face.

Frank had been listening from another room.

"Thank you for sticking up for me Joan; you look delighted with yourself," he said, coming in and giving her a hug.

"I am. I've wanted to put Jane Manners in her place for years," she said, smiling.

Jane Manners had taught all the Cartland children, and none of them liked her very much.

"Now, if you've really left school, you can make yourself useful around here. Start by washing those dishes and pans, and then you can clean the cottage windows".

With no school to attend, Frank dedicated his time to labouring in the forge, a task he disliked, and on the farms, an activity he found joy in. Despite the initial disappointment of not finding anyone willing to let him mend their broken cycle, he persisted, asking anyone he saw with a bike. His determination paid off when the butcher Alan Pope, tired of Frank's daily inquiries, finally relented.

"Let's see what you can do with this old thing; it's been in the shed for over a year."

Mr. Pope pulled out a battered, old, black bike with a buckled wheel from the back of his garden shed.

"Thanks," said Frank excitedly. "I'll make it like new."

With sweating effort, Frank pushed the old, rusty bike back to the forge. He began working on it in the evenings after John had left for the pub. Each night, he dedicated four hours to the task. By the end of the week, he had completely rebuilt the bike. He proudly returned a shiny black, fully functional bike to the surprised butcher.

"Well done, Frank," he said, "here's a bob for your hard work."

"Thank you, Mr. Pope," Frank said, his voice filled with genuine gratitude. His eyes sparkled with a mix of pride and appreciation as he accepted the reward for his hard work.

Frank was delighted. It was the first money he had ever earned. Then it was back to work in the forge until he could find another broken bike to fix.

When the fire pit was roaring, the heat from the forge was oppressive and hot enough to blister your skin if you got too close to it. The constant noise from John's hammers striking the anvil was deafening. The hiss of hot metal as John dipped it into cold-water buckets sounded like a basket full of angry snakes. If there is a hell, this must be what it will be like, thought Frank, wiping away the stinging sweat that constantly ran into his eyes.

The Reverend Sexton was always preaching that his parishioners would all be cast into the fires of hell if they strayed from Christian ways. Frank didn't believe it even as he worked in this hot, dark place.

A small piece of hot coal spat from the fire pit and burnt his hand. *I have had enough of this*, he suddenly thought.

"Hey, where the hell are you going?" shouted John as he watched Frank take off his leather apron and walk towards the forge's door.

"Sorry, John. I can't work here any longer. You'll have to get someone else to do your dirty work," Frank bravely replied.

"Well, fuck off, you little runt," was the loud and sharp reply from his big, angry brother.
Frank managed to duck out of the solid oak forge door before a giant black horseshoe smashed into it with a loud thud.

Back in the cottage, he explained to Joan that he had had enough of forge work and told her John's reaction to his leaving.

"I'll try to calm him down. I'm sure he'll get someone else to help, but make sure you stay out of his way for a while," a worried Joan replied.

Frank had no intention of going anywhere near his increasingly disturbing older brother.

Chapter Four

Now that he had escaped the forge and John, Frank went to find more work with the local farmers, particularly enjoying the summer harvesting. Fascinated with anything mechanical, especially the new steam powered threshing machines, he took every opportunity to help with repairs. A swift learner, he soon had many of the villagers saying,

"Get Frank Cartland to help. He can fix anything". Following his success at rebuilding the butcher's bike, more people began to ask Frank to repair their bikes, and his reputation as a fixer grew. Then Frank fell in love for the first time.

Farmer Albert Betts had a wire-haired fox terrier bitch called Lucky, who followed Frank all over the farm. Lucky had another litter of puppies in the autumn, much to Farmer Betts' disgust.

"There are more than enough bloody animals around here already," he told Frank, picking up an empty hessian potato sack. "I'm going to have to drown this lot."

"No, you won't", said Frank boldly, snatching the sack from the farmer. "I'll find homes for them." There were only three in the litter, and Frank decided it would be easy to find homes for the puppies. Anyway, he wanted the smallest puppy for himself. It was the runt of the litter, noticeably smaller than its two bossy sisters, with coarse salt and pepper-coloured hair that stuck out at right angles all over his body. He looked lopsided, with one little ear folded over and the other standing straight up. Looking down into the innocent, big brown eyes of this funny little dog, Frank said,

"Think I'll call you Spike." Spike jumped up and licked his face.

Frank did find homes for the two bitches. The spinster sisters of the local butcher, Mabel and Sarah Coles, had just lost their old dog and were delighted to give the puppies a new home.

At first, the rest of the Cartland family were unhappy with the new addition.

"Another bloody mouth to feed," was John's reaction.

"He's only small and won't eat much. He can share my food," said Frank.

John just glared at him. Fortunately for Frank, his big brother had found a strong young local lad to help in the forge. John had told Frank,

"You were a lazy sod. This kid is a real worker."

Before long, Spike's friendly nature and funny looks won everyone over. Even John gave Spike the occasional old bone. There was also an unexpected bonus from having Spike around—no more rats in the forge. Rats were always a problem in the village, especially after harvest time. Large brown rats scurrying along the edges of buildings, barns, and churches were a common site.

Being a terrier, Spike was born to kill these rodents. Unfortunately, he would also chase anything else that ran away from him. Rabbits and cats soon learnt to keep well clear of him.

However, an incident with Spike did cost Frank some money.

Spike's reputation as a rat catcher became widely known in the village, and one day, neighbour Will Cooper asked Frank to take the dog into his garden. Mrs Cooper had gone to collect the eggs early one morning from the nesting boxes, and as she lifted the box lid, a large rat had jumped out. Rumour had it that villagers all over Burlham heard her screams.

"There's a rat's nest somewhere behind the chicken run." Will Cooper said to Frank. Now, his wife's experience meant he had to get rid of it quickly. It didn't take Spike long to find the nest. He was soon scraping away, his front paws digging wildly and throwing earth out in all directions behind him.

Uncovering the nest, Spike made short work of the mother rat. Grabbing the nape of the rat's neck, the dog violently shook it, breaking the neck instantly. After killing the remaining rats, Spike was tired, panting happily, and muddy, and he had a couple of bleeding rat bites on his nose.

"Well done, Spike," said Frank as he pulled him away from the remains of the rats.

"That's a good job finished. Let's go home for some tea."

They were just passing the front of the chicken coop when a nosey chicken poked its head through the bars. Instinctively, Spike snapped his jaws and bit the poor chicken's head clean off. Blood sprayed wildly from the headless bird, covering Spike and the neighbour's trousers. Mr. Cooper had just come out of his house to congratulate them.

Will Cooper's mood changed instantly.

"Get that dangerous little mutt away from here," he shouted after them.

Frank and Spike were already running for home.

Although he had been pleased to get rid of the rats, Will Cooper was unhappy to lose one of his best-laying hens. Frank had to buy a replacement hen from Albert

Betts. Still, as consolation, the Cartland family had a lovely, fat chicken for Sunday dinner that week.
Spike was given the parson's nose.

Two weeks later, Joe, on one of his trips home, said,
"Let's go to the Railway Arms for a drink, Frank."
The pub was next to the railway station, far away from the main village. It was the place where all the village youngsters went for a drink. The landlord, Dan Turner, had a flexible approach to underage drinking. With the pub being away from the centre of the village, it was easy to see when Constable Clarke was on his rounds and cycling down the road towards the pub.
Joe brought a pint of mild for himself and a half for his young brother. Spike loved beer and had his own ashtray full, which he lapped up.
Sharing a packet of pork scratching's with Frank; he was a happy little terrier.
Joe and Frank were sitting in the corner of the pub smoking their Woodbines when the older one said,
"How'd you like to earn a bit of extra money?"
"Of course, I would, but what would I have to do for it?" replied Frank a little warily.
"Be the bookie's runner for our village," said Joe.
Growing up close to the Newmarket horse racing industry, Frank knew what a bookie's runner was - he also knew that being a runner was illegal.
"How much will I get?" Frank asked.
"That depends on how good you are," said Joe.
Most of the villages around Newmarket used bookie's runners. They were usually young boys running around the village to collect money from the men and a

few women looking to place a bet. The boys would then deliver all the bets to a local village pub. When he had all that day's bets, the landlord would send them on to their bookmakers in Newmarket.

Frank turned out to be an outstanding runner, although he came close to being caught by PC Clarke on several occasions. As he would later admit, Constable Clarke often turned a bit of a blind eye to Frank's activities. He liked an occasional bet himself and disagreed with this law restricting gambling.

Within a few months of being a runner, Frank had saved enough money to buy a rusty old green bike from Dan Turner. He then spent hours stripping the bike down, repainting it dark green with some paint he found in the forge, and then rebuilding it with his trademark, attention to detail. On the front of the bike, he had fixed a wire basket for Spike to sit in. They didn't need a bell; Spike would bark at anyone who got in the way as they tore around the dusty village paths and lanes on the bike his brother Joe named 'The Green Flash'.

The freedom the old bike gave him opened Frank's world. Working hard, he became a bookie's runner for two nearby villages and Burlham. However, this additional work was to cause him some problems.

There was a lad called Tommy Dunn who lived in the next village, Farewell. Tommy had been the bookie's runner for the village but was slow-witted and sometimes 'mislaid' a few bets. The landlords of the two Farewell pubs had lost patience with him, and after hearing of Frank's growing reputation, they sacked Tommy and gave Frank the job.

"I'll get that cocky little bastard, Frank Cartland, he's taken me bloody job," said Tommy Dunn to his mates.

Frank and Spike came charging through the right-hand bend into Farewell the following Saturday morning. Frank was pedalling at full speed. There, in the middle of the road, was a giant tangle of tree branches and on the bank nearby stood Tommy Dunn and two of his gang, Fred and Sam.

"Watch this. He can't miss all those branches," squeaked an excited Tommy as Frank approached.

Frank snatched the brakes but couldn't stop. The rear wheel locked, and the bike swerved sideways. Poor old Spike flew out of his basket. One of the branches then went through the bike's front wheel, locking it and pitching Frank over the handlebars. He landed hard on the road, with the bike crashing down on top of him. The brake lever caught Frank on his forehead slicing the skin open down to his left eyebrow. There was a lot of blood. He lay unmoving on the grey hard surface. Dazed, but conscious. Gathering his muddled thoughts, Frank decided he had had a lot worse. Tommy and his mates came down from the bank laughing. They gathered around Frank's prone, dirty, and bloody figure to admire their handiwork.

"I think you've killed him," said Sam a little nervously.

Frank lay still. He had been in similar situations before. Slightly opening one eye, he saw the dusty, scuffed toecap of Tommy Dunn's hobnail boot. It was only six inches away from his face.

"Nah, he's only pretending; that'll wake him up," said Tommy as he lifted his foot to kick Frank.

Just in time, a furious Spike arrived. He had been lucky: he landed in a soft, mossy ditch when he flew. Scrambling out of it onto the bank, unhurt. Looking around, he saw the boys surrounding Frank. He immediately launched himself straight for them - snarling, biting, and snapping at their legs.

The three boys panicked and scattered, but not before Spike managed to get a few sound bites into them. The best one had been into Tommy's calf, just before his foot reached Frank. After chasing the boys right away, Spike went back to Frank and started licking the blood from his face.

"Thanks for your help, old boy," said Frank as he slowly and stiffly pulled himself off the road. Checking over his arms and legs, Frank found he was scraped and bloodied, but nothing seemed to be broken. He inspected his buckled front bike wheel as PC Clarke cycled around the corner.

"What the hell have you been doing, Frank? Have you knocked down a tree?"

When Frank explained what had happened, PC Clarke said adamantly:

"You leave that little bugger to me. Now get yourself home, and Joan will clean you up." Frank hobbled away, pushing his damaged bike with Spike trotting by his side.

I've got a spare wheel. We can be back on the road by Monday, he soon decided.

"What on earth have you done this time?" asked Joan when she saw her bloodied, limping little brother.

"Just fallen off my bike," said Frank. "I'll be fine." But the concern for her young brother had managed to etch another worry line into Joan's forehead.

Frank would become quite proud of the scar on his forehead, which spread down to his eyebrow. It remained with him his whole life. Most of the time, it was faint, but it turned pink and noticeable whenever Frank became angry.

PC Clarke had cycled straight to Tommy Dunn's house. He knew the way, having had to call there many times before. Arthur Dunn, Tommy's father, was well known to him. Occasionally, he had to arrest Arthur for fighting on Saturday nights. This was often after a heavy session in the pub when he had won some money on the horses.

Tommy stood crying, standing on the table in the Dunn's kitchen, while his mother bandaged up his bleeding leg.

"That bloody dog of Frank Cartland attacked me for no reason. It needs fucking shooting, "squealed Tommy.

"I'll go and finish off that scraggy little mutt," his father said, taking his shotgun from the wall. At that moment, PC Clarke walked into their kitchen.

"Hold on a minute, Arthur," he said, "put that gun down unless you want some real trouble."

Then, despite Tommy's protests of innocence, Constable Clarke gave the Dunn family the actual story. Tommy received a couple of tough cuffs on the head from his father and peed his pants. Arthur Dunn dragged his crying son upstairs to his room and locked him in there for the rest of the day.

Tommy Dunn gave Frank no further trouble. But there was plenty of trouble to come. 1914 arrived, and soon everyone's lives changed forever.

Chapter Five

By March 1914, Frank had set himself up as a cycle repairer. After some pleading from Joan, John had reluctantly allowed him to base himself in a small corner of the forge. Noticing Frank painting an old plank of wood one day in early March, John asked,
"What you're doin?"
"I'm making a sign for my new business," said Frank, proudly holding up the plank. The plank had a dark green background, and CARTLAND CYCLES was written on it in bright yellow paint.
"You can't bloody write any good, so how'd you make it?" said John.
"Doctor Jones helped me," replied Frank.
"Just don't be getting that metal crap in my way, or I'll melt 'em down in the forge, bloody things," said John before stomping off to the pub.
Early one chilly April morning, Frank was repairing a broken bicycle in his corner of the forge when he heard the distinctive, sharp sound of a single-cylinder engine outside. Doctor Howard Jones had purchased a new Triumph motorcycle and was keen to show it off.
"That's the most beautiful thing I've ever seen," said Frank after rushing outside. Admiring the silver machine, he added.
"It's a 4 hp 550cc type B model with a fixed-belt drive, and it costs £49."
Doctor Jones had been giving Frank motoring magazines, and Frank had learnt by heart all the details of each motorbike and motorcar.
"Frank, you already know more about the motorbike than I do," laughed Doctor Jones, "but

actually, it only cost me £45."

Momentarily depressed, Frank thought he'd never have enough money to afford a motorbike like that.

Doctor Jones had witnessed Charlie Cartland's treatment of Frank in those early years and was amazed at the happy, hard-working young man he was developing into. Whenever he had the chance, he would encourage Frank's interest in mechanical things.

"Come on, jump on the back. Let's go for a spin," the doctor said to the young man.

Without hesitation, Frank jumped on. Unused to the extra weight on his motorbike, Doctor Jones slowly moved off. Frank soon urged him to go faster.

Buzzing with excitement from this first motorised experience, Frank realised that bicycles would never be quick enough for him again.

By July 1914, everyone knew the war with Germany was a reality. Still, in the small country villages of England, it had little immediate impact. The war was just something that was happening hundreds of miles away, across the sea—almost another world.

Frank's business of repairing bikes continued to grow, and just a day before his birthday, when the Triumph engine broke down, Doctor Jones allowed him to rebuild it.

"Here's an early birthday present for you," he said. "See if you can fix it."

Frank dismantled the damaged engine and, using the new parts Doctor Jones had purchased, lovingly rebuilt it with great care. He refitted the engine into the frame of the Triumph and nervously, with Doctor Jones, John, and

Joan looking on, worked the kick starter. The engine burst into life instantly.

Joan sighed with relief as Doctor Jones jumped on and roared off to test it. He had been gone for more than ten minutes when Frank started to worry. Then, with great joy he watched the silver Triumph reappear around the corner. Doctor Jones stopped the bike in front of them and, with a great smile on his face, said:

"Amazing. Frank, it runs better than ever. You have magic in your fingers." John walked away in disgust.

At that moment, Frank realised he wanted to spend the rest of his life building engines.

"I just love being able to create a living, breathing machine from all those colds, metal bits," he enthused to Joan and anyone else who would listen.

"But look at your fingers, Frank. You have cut them to ribbons on that sharp, hard metal," Joan said with concern.

'That's fine. It doesn't hurt. I'm always going to leave a bit of my blood behind when I build an engine. It will show it's one of mine!" Frank laughed.

The army recruitment campaign didn't reach the shires until 1915. On a hot August Saturday, an army brass band, a symbol of patriotism and unity, arrived in Burlham.

"Come and look at the band and soldiers," said an excited Joe, who had come home for the weekend, to his sister Joan. She was in the outhouse doing the family washing.

Reluctantly, she joined the rest of the excited villagers as they gathered outside the village hall to hear the band perform.

When the band had finished playing their stirring marching tunes, an immaculately dressed sergeant major addressed the happy crowd.

"We are here to offer all you fine young men the opportunity to join all the other brave English soldiers. To come and fight for your country to defeat the Hun," he proclaimed in a commanding voice, emphasizing the courage and valour of the potential recruits" Then, smiling at the captivated crowd, he added:

"And remember lads, every girl loves a man in uniform." He pointed to a handsome young sergeant seated behind a trestle table on the corner of the lawn.

All single men 18 and over were encouraged to sign, although conscription would not come for another year. Of course, Frank's age of 15 meant he wasn't old enough to sign up.

Much to Joan's distress, her sweetheart Norman Crowe and her brother Joe excitedly joined the long queue of young Burlham men. Despite Joan's pleading, they had both enlisted and joined the Cambridge Regiment within the hour. Seeing his sister cry constantly upset Frank. To lighten the mood, he said,

"At least you won't have to do all of Joe's smelly washing for a while."

This set off a new wave of tears from Joan.

Norman and Joe had become great mates, even though Norman was four years older than Joe. They all knew he loved Joan and one day would pluck up the courage to ask her to marry him.

"When I was your age, Norman took me down to the Railway Arms for my first drink and gave me my first Woodbine," Joe had told Frank.

They were happy to join the army together and looked forward to the adventure, but the unknown dangers that lay ahead cast a shadow of uncertainty. Of course, none of these boys and young men knew the horrors they would soon face.

"Have to learn me some French if I'm going to chat up some of those lovely French girls, but don't worry, sis, I'll look after your Norman," said Joe, giving Norman a sly wink and Joan a big hug. Norman kept quiet; his mother stood beside Joan, distressed, and crying. Suddenly, he took Joan's hand and said,

"Joanie, when I come back, will you marry me?"

With tears streaming down her cheeks, Joan said,

"Of course, I will, Norman Crowe, you silly man. I love you." Then she hugged him until his ribs hurt.

"I'm going nowhere. It's not bloody worth it," said John, much to Joan's relief.

He knew he had responsibilities at home and always worked long, hard hours in the forge. But really, he had no intention of giving up his evenings at The Red Lion drinking… one of many ways in which he was increasing like his father.

Two months later, Frank stood silently, Spike sitting next to him. His crying sisters and sullen brother were alongside him as Joe and Norman proudly marched away. The boys all looked so grown up in their new army uniforms, their shiny black polished boots and the metal on their brown rifles glinting in the weak autumn sun. The column of fine young men filed past, and Joe shouted over his shoulder,

"Look after our sisters, Frank. We will be back soon, so don't worry about us."

An unsmiling Norman waved and blew Joan a kiss. They would never see Norman again, and Joe would return as a stranger. Joan's heart ached with the knowledge that their lives would never be the same. After training in Yorkshire, the Cambridge Regiment, which included around 50 officers and 1000 men, crossed the English Channel to France in January 1916. Joan had been receiving letters regularly from Joe and Norman, and from the tone of the letters, it was clear they were both in exceptionally good spirits. Of course, Joe's letters were optimistic and told of his adventures with the French girls.

Norman's letters were typically reserved, focusing on topics like the countryside and weather. Nevertheless, he managed to express how much he missed Joan, loved her, and looked forward to returning home. He always referred to his fiancée as "my Joanie."

In the last letters she received in May 1916, Norman had said that all the boys in the regiment were getting excited because they had been told they would soon be moved to the frontline on the Somme. That was the last letter Joan received from her lover.

Joe and Norman were looking forward to some action. They had been training for months and, together with all their comrades, were desperate to do their duty - without question. The regiments were moved up to the front-line trenches on the Somme during June. The snaking column of thousands of men had marched to the artillery's constant, deafening sound.

"Bloody hell this is a mess." Were Joe's first words to Norman when they reached their billet in the front-line trench. Norman screwed up his nose as a large brown rat scurried passed his muddy army boot.

Their Sargent arrived carrying two shovels. He thrust one at each of them.

"Cartland and Crowe, follow me. New latrines need digging."

Frank will laugh when he hears I've got the shit job again. Thought Joe as they followed the Sargent through the labyrinth of trenches to the new laterite site.

With time to kill, tempers among the young men thrown together in these dirty claustrophobic trenches, often led to fights. Joe ending up with a black eye after one of his cocky, sharp remarks.

Norman kept very much to himself, spending his time writing a letter to Joan and thinking of home. After much re-writing this is the final version, she would eventually know by heart. He wrote.

My dear Joanie

I'm writing this from my narrow bunk in our shelter cut into the back of the main trench. Ten of us are crammed in here, and it's hard to get any sleep what with the constant shelling, snoring and other noises from the lads all around me.

Joe is happy, playing cards and laughing most of the time. He mixes much better than I do.

I hope all is good at home. I hear the weather has been kind, which should mean the wheat will be growing strong.

They say this madness should all be over next month. Rumor is that we will go over the top in a few days. I am so looking forward to being back with you and helping Farmer Bye harvest all the fields of golden corn.

You know it's my favourite time of the year. Then it would be wonderful if we could get married in

September. I will leave you to talk to the vicar. Expect we will have to live with mother for a short while but soon we should have a place of our own.

Signing off now as Joe wants me to join him in the cards.

Your even loving Norman.

This was a letter Joan didn't receive until Norman's belongings were returned to his mother months later. Once Mrs Crowe had given the letter to her the pain of Norman's death reminded raw for her whole life. Joan kept it in a tin box under her bed and read it daily, each night placing a kiss on his name.

In later years the letter became little more than a worn scrap of yellowed paper, with the writing faded away. But of course, this didn't matter, Joan knew everyone of its two hundred and three words by heart.

During the weeks of June 1940, the German lines had been shelled mercilessly. The British commanders were supremely confident, to the point of arrogance, that the constant bombardment would have severely weakened the German forces.

From the British headquarters a mile behind the front line the Commander-in-Chief Sir Henry Rawlinson announced

"Prepare the men, weather conditions are improving, we start the advance tomorrow morning."
There was a muttering of surprise from the Commanders gathered.

"Are we sure enough damage has been done to the German guns." It was the question from one of them.

"This order is directly from Commander Haig; do you think you should question it."

The response and the look from Rawlinson silenced any further remarks.

The British Commanders were confident that the German frontline would be unable to resist the new planned offensive. Evidence of that arrogance came when an order was sent down the lines.

They must be mad.

Captain Ronald Hardy swore to himself when he received the order he must pass on to his men. He called all his sergeants together.

"Walk? Are you sure Sir." Questioned Sergeant Barry Jones of the Cambridge Regiment when they were given the order.

"These are our orders, now go and give your troops the good news." Was Captain Hardy's reply, attempting to display more confidence than he felt. "Right, you bloody horrible bunch. When the whistle blasts you will leave these trenches and take a steady walk towards the |Hun." Barry Jones told his platoon.

"Sounds like this is going to be easy," said Joe to some of his mates when they heard about the order.

7am 1st July 1916

"Looks like blood in the sky." Said Norman to Joe as they emerged from their bunks at sunrise.

For the first time in three days the sky was clear, heat from the warming sun causing a light mist to rise from the drying ground.

Joe and Norman stood together nervously waiting at the base of the wooden ladders they would use to leave the safety of the trench.

"Get ready," the call came from their sergeant. The friends crushed their last, half-smoked Woodbines under their boots into the soft, grey trench mud. Then, they clasped their hands and smiled at each other.

"Don't forget you owe me a beer. It's your round when we get home," said Joe. "I bought the last one at the Railway Arms."

Norman grinned, but he was not smiling when, with his hand still tightly held in Joe's, he said:

"Tell Joanie I love her."

"You can tell her yourself when we get back, mate," replied Joe, but he had also stopped smiling.

For more than a minute, the gathered soldiers were completely still. Thousands of men holding their breaths.

Suddenly, the silence was broken by a hysterical shriek as hundreds of whistles blew all along the line. On mass, thousands of young British men rose and went out onto the stark grey, muddy wastelands to start their walk of death.

Joe slipped on the wet mud as he left the trench, but Norman didn't. His long legs had taken him to the top of the ladder first and the moment he stood to start the slow advance he was hit by a hail of machine gun fire. His body danced like a demented stringed puppet, and then, falling sideways, smashed into Joe. The impact knocked Joe back down into the trench. As he fell backwards, his metal helmet slipped off. Joe's head crashed into the wooden walkway so hard that his skull fractured on impact. He was instantly knocked out.

He'd been saved from slaughter by his dead best friend.

Slaughter it certainly was. Within minutes, thousands of dead and desperately injured men lay upon the once-green fields of the Somme. A monstrous German scythe had instantly and totally felled British youth's fresh, green shoots.

"Over here, this one is still alive." shouted a medic when he found Joe.

"Give me a hand to lift him."

Joe was unconscious and wholly soaked in Norman's blood. Lifting Norman's lifeless body off Joe they could see his chest moving. Gently the medics placed him onto a stretcher. With so much blood covering him, they were convinced he must have a significant injury somewhere.

At the field hospital, Joe's blood-soaked clothes were carefully cut away, but no injuries were found. All the blood had belonged to Norman Crowe.

The newspapers back in England that week were full of headlines.

"Our boys slaughtered"

"Massacre on the Somme"

With no news from Joe, Norman, or any other boys who had left with them, the village of Burlham was in limbo. The residents spent each day just waiting and thinking the worst.

"I know we won't see them again," said Joan constantly.

The worry and stress had seen her lose almost two stone in weight. She had hardly eaten or slept since the last letters from her boys.

"Their letters will probably have been lost," said Frank without much conviction. "I'm sure we'll hear from them soon."

For most women and girls in the village, the short walk up the hill to St Mary's church became a daily ritual. Joan spent many hours in the family pew just praying, constantly kneeling on the cold stone church floor, which turned her knees cherry red.

The letters arrived on 28th July. Dawn had brought a beautiful, clear, blue summer morning sky. It was also Frank's 17th birthday.

Joan saw the postman's bike approaching and let out a low moan as if she knew he had a letter for her that would begin, "We regret to inform you ..."

John ran out, snatched the letter from the postman, and tore it open.

"He's not dead," he said, handing the letter to Joan.

"What does it say?" asked Frank. He was desperate to know what had happened to his brother.

With a trembling voice, Joan read,

"Private Joe Cartland has received a serious head injury and is in a French hospital." Excitedly, she added, "They will send him home in about two weeks."

Putting the letter down, she burst into happy sobs. They all looked at each other with relief; even John slightly smiled.

But it was just two minutes of happiness. Their mood changed when Norman's mother, a hysterical Mrs. Crowe, burst into the cottage. The letter she waved confirmed that her son, Joan's sweetheart, had been killed.

"...died bravely in the line of duty."

This was the letter Joan had been expecting. Frank would forever remember the tears and sorrow that lasted throughout his terrible birthday. It was a scene played out in many towns, villages, and hamlets throughout Great Britain in that most sombre of summers. Cricket on the sunny village greens held no attraction that summer. Many villages no longer had enough young men to form an entire team.

Twenty thousand men and boys were killed on that one day, 1st July 1916, at the Somme. Five of those were from Burlham.

The extreme emotions Joan experienced in those few minutes - finding out that her brother was still alive and that her lover was dead - were too much and caused her complete collapse. She never really recovered from that day, although through necessity, she continued to look after the Cartland household as before. Joan had never been an optimistic person. Circumstances meant her whole life had to be devoted to others. Her life had never been her own. The rest of her family always took priority.

Now, the one chance to find happiness for herself had gone, and any lightness of spirit she had previously felt had left her forever. Norman Crowe's body never returned to his home village. He was buried along with thousands of other young men in one of the many war cemeteries close to the Somme.

The Reverend Walter Sexton organised a memorial service for Albert and the four other Burlham boys killed in the war. The whole village attended the service. A brass plaque was dedicated and engraved with their names and placed on the right-hand side of the church wall, close to the Cartland pew. This, at least, gave Joan and the other families some comfort and a focus for their grieving.

Frank had always loved Joe. He had admired and looked up to him his whole life. When Joe eventually arrived home two months later, Frank was shocked to see that only the shell of the cocky, happy young man who had marched away so confidently just one year ago remained.

It broke Frank's heart to see the change in his brother, who sat silently by the kitchen range day after long day, not talking and just gently rocking back and forth.

Tearfully, he told Joan, "I can't bear to watch him, I want the old Joe back,".

"I know, we all do, but at least he is alive," she said with a bitterness Frank hadn't heard before.

"Sorry, Joan, I didn't think. I know you miss Norman badly."

Joan said nothing. She just gave Frank a big, long hug. Doctor Jones, into whose care Joe had been placed, explained to Joan that when Joe fell back into the trench, his head had fallen directly onto the end of a broken wooden stake. Skull fragments had been pushed into his brain and would be lodged there for the rest of his life. No one could be sure just how much of his brain had been damaged or how much of a recovery he would make.

For the first time in his life, Frank experienced emotional pain, then real anger, as he witnessed the distress this war had brought to his family and the families of his friends. All his life, he had looked forward to spring. It made him optimistic, especially the sudden explosion of golden daffodils waving in the warming sun.

Almost overnight, they would banish winter memories as they turned everything yellow, spreading their bright light haphazardly throughout the village. But this year, these beautiful flowers' three to four-week lifespan held little joy; their short, bright life depressed him.

Only Spike managed to bring back something of the old Joe. Spike would often sit with him—it was as if he could sense Joe's pain. Often, he would jump onto his lap and lick his face, which usually brought a rare smile to Joe's lips.

"Why don't you take Spike for a walk?" said Frank to Joe one bright April day. To his own and Joan's delight, Joe had replied,

I ... I think I will today. Come on, old boy." "Don't go far," said a worried Joan.

Two hours later, the family was becoming concerned. There was no sign of Joe or Spike.

"I'll go and look for them. I think I know where they would have gone," said Frank, jumping onto one of his bikes. He cycled through the village and out towards the Devil's Dyke.

These ancient earthworks dominated the landscape for more than ten miles and divided the Burlham and Farewell parishes. The Devil's Dyke ran through the racecourse at Newmarket Heath and provided a good and popular view of the racing. Frank reached the dyke and noticed the black outline of Joe and Spike on the skyline. They were walking towards him. Frank was relieved to see Joe looking so happy, with Spike panting at his side. Greeting him, an excited Joe said:

"We walked along to the racecourse and watched some of the horses. Spike has been chasing rabbits." In the following years, a walk to the racecourse would become a regular event for Joe and Spike, but Joe never became mentally fit enough to work again.

On bad days, severe headaches would confine him to his bed, and these became more frequent in later years. Frank occasionally suffered a pang of jealousy since

Spike had transferred most of his affection to Joe. But he had to smile one day as he watched the pair wander off down the lane to the Railway Arms for their daily ration of beer. As they went, Spike turned his head and looked back at Frank as if to say, "Don't worry; I'll look after him."

Early November morning, a dusty and bruised Doctor Jones entered Frank's workshop.

"I left the old Triumph outside for you, Frank," he said. "It's got damaged forks this time. I've fallen off for the last time. If I ride it again, I'll probably kill myself, so it's about time I got a car instead. You can have the bike."

"Are you sure?" Frank asked. "I'll pay you for it."

"No, that's not necessary, but you can give me a free service on the car when I get it," Doctor Jones replied.

Frank couldn't help himself. He gave the doctor a big hug.

"Careful lad, my ribs hurt enough already", the doctor had protested.

Frank soon had the Triumph running sweetly again and took every opportunity to ride it. Before long, he had become a skilled rider and an expert motorbike repairer.

Rushing around Cambridgeshire's villages and country lanes became a drug to him. The freedom and excitement this gave him was unequalled by anything else he had ever experienced.

Of course, he knew about the daring exploits of the racing motorcyclists at The Isle of Man and Brooklands, having absorbed all the motoring magazines supplied by Doctor Jones. Now, he had just one ambition in life—to join them.

Chapter Six

By 1917, with the war showing no sign of ending, Frank was determined to enlist. He felt a strong need, in some way, to avenge Norman's death and the mental destruction of his brother. But he knew it would be difficult to tell his sister.

"You are so selfish," protested Joan. "Hasn't there been enough pain in our family already? You are too young, not yet eighteen and only older men are being conscripted."

"I'm sorry, Joan, it's… it's just something I need to do," replied Frank. Despite Joan's despair and protests, he was determined to enlist.

Although he didn't want Frank to go to join the war, Doctor Jones had heard that there was a need for motorcycle dispatch riders in the army. He called on Joan and Frank at the forge to tell them.

"I thought Frank would be interested if he were still determined to sign up," he said, looking at Joan.

"That sounds really great. It would be the best job for me," said Frank excitedly.

Joan said nothing for a while but thought this must be safer than being an ordinary infantryman like Joe and poor Norman had been.

"Thank you for your interest, Doctor Jones. If that's what Frank wants, I can't stop him," she said, tears welling in her eyes.

"Th…That's alright Joan."

Howard Jones's instinct had been to put his arms around Joan, but his shyness caused the moment to pass.

Howard found the right contacts in the army, and Frank soon signed up as a dispatch rider.

On 1st August, just four days after his eighteenth birthday, Frank arrived in France.

Reporting for duty at the motor pool, he was issued with his army motorbike. Frank was delighted to learn it was a Triumph Model H Roadster, widely known as the "Trusty Triumph."

Evidently, the bike had seen plenty of action already—its army-green paint was severely chipped and scarred with what looked like shrapnel marks.

"Who was riding this old thing before me," Frank asked his sergeant.

"Never mind, Sonny. It's your bike now. All you have to do is ride the bloody thing." This was all his superior would say. No one else seemed to know the bike's history, either…or they were reluctant to tell him.

Doing the thing he loved best, Frank had impressed the army instructors with his riding skills, his complete lack of fear and his engineering expertise. His reputation quickly became widespread, and Frank was often given the most hazardous assignments.

The daily routine of taking dispatches from the British Generals' château headquarters, which were safely behind the lines, to the frontline trenches became second nature to him. At the frontline, he had an introduction to the terrible destruction and the squalid conditions three years of war had already brought.

At night, he would lay in his narrow bunk, unable to sleep because he was thinking about the horrors all around him. Now, knowing how his brother had felt, he thought. *How can anything be worth all this misery and pain?*

One dispatch gave him many sleepless nights and left him with memories that would remain with him all his life.

It was dusk, and the grey light was fading fast. Frank had been riding through driving, cold rain, and German shelling, which became particularly heavy as he approached the frontline.

Unable to see more than a few yards, he decided to take shelter. Frank stopped the bike outside an abandoned old barn that had somehow survived the shells that had destroyed the farmhouse that had once stood next to it. He stepped inside the dark building, relieved to be out of the rain as his eyes struggled to adjust to the darkness.

The barn had no windows. Only a narrow shaft of light came from a jagged hole blown into the roof. Frank had walked two paces into the dark barn when the overpowering smell hit him like a punch in the face. It was all the worst smells of his childhood - a mix of rotting meat, shit and piss. Then he heard a noise which sounded like the neighbour's pigs back home feeding in their pen. He turned on his army torch.

In the far corner of the barn, he could make out movement and took out his pistol. The beam of light from the torch settled on a site of nightmares. Six or seven fat brown rats were feasting on and in the remains of a human body. He could just recognise the dark-blue uniform of a French infantryman. Frank lost control and hysterically fired his pistol into the heaving mass. The rats scattered, and, in the torchlight, he watched a swarm of big, black buzzing flies as it appeared, snake-like, out of the body.

Retching, Frank turned and staggered out to his Triumph. Despite the falling shells and hard, driving rain, he started the engine and roared away. After that experience, seeing rats or large black flies filled him with disgust and horror.

One week later, still unsettled and depressed after encountering the rats, an unusually dry day saw him riding through a badly rutted road that followed a small river.

The beat of the single-cylinder Triumph engine was constant as he scrambled along the uneven track. The words hammering through his head reflected Frank's mood.

Noise, mud, blood, and death
Noise, mud, blood, and death
Noise, mud, blood, and death and
the beat went on and on...

Frank was hot, depressed and extremely tired. The slimy mud had dried in places to become gritty, grey dust. It had invaded his clothes, eyes, nose, and hair. To his left, he noticed the sun twinkling on the water. Between the trees flashing by, he could see a small silver river - no more than twenty feet wide - flowing with a slow current.

Braking to a stop, Frank got off the Triumph and leant the bike against a willow tree growing at the river's edge. Its long branches caressed the clear, silver water as it flowed past. He was surprised to find that the willow tree made him think about his father and cricket for just a fleeting moment. Then, the thought had gone.

The water looked irresistibly inviting. It was the first time in the six months since arriving in France that Frank had seen water without light-grey scum, dead horses and bloated bodies floating along it. Within seconds, he had stripped off his dusty clothes and was naked. The bank was steep and slippery, so Frank carefully slid into the clear water. The water was icy cold and no more than four feet deep at its centre, but he didn't care. Diving down, he immersed himself, feeling free and clean for the first time since leaving England.

As his head cleared the water, he opened his eyes and noticed a young woman standing on the bank. She was under the willow tree next to his clothes and watching him. For many seconds, they stood staring at each other, and then she said,
"Bonjour, parlez-vous Français?"

Frozen and struck dumb, Frank stood as the current of the water flowed around the thighs of his shivering body. He tried to hide his manhood with his hands, though actually, with the icy water, it was more like his boyhood, and he needed only one hand to hide his embarrassment.

Frank had picked up the odd word of French, and coming to his senses, he replied,

"Bonjour, Madame, mon nom est Frank."

"Mon nom est Marie," replied the girl. She was smiling as she speedily stepped out of her dress and slip. Naked, she slipped down the bank into the water and slowly walked towards Frank. Marie was about five feet tall and very slim. Her auburn hair was long and curled up as it rested on her shoulders.

Conkers, her hair is the colour of conkers. It had been his favourite game as a boy. He once had a tenner, which he retired after it won ten brutal contests. He had removed its string and placed it carefully on the ledge above the range in the forge cottage kitchen. *I wonder if it's still there*, he thought.

The next moment, he was being splashed with cold water. Marie was close to him now, and her infectious light giggle made him laugh for the first time in years. He noticed that his new friend's smile seemed to take over her whole face and that her small, firm breasts had dark brown, hard nipples. She came closer and continued to splash him. Frank splashed her back before grabbing her. They fell together under the water and spent idyllic minutes playing and laughing in this magical stream before Marie took his hand and led him back to shore. They struggled up the steep slope before she pushed Frank down on the bank under the lime-green leaves of the old willow tree.

The long, soft grass enclosed him like a glove. Marie opened her legs and slid down on top of him. He could feel the hard bone above her dark, brown-haired mound pressing into him. Her hair, smelling of wood smoke, enclosed his head like a canopy. Urgently, she rubbed her wet body against his, her bullet-like nipples pressed hard, almost painfully, into his chest. Gradually, they warmed each other, and as she moved, riding him like a horse, Frank quickly became aroused enough to enter her and lost himself in the exquisite experience. As she moved, her ride became a trot, which soon became a canter and a furious, reckless gallop. When Frank exploded inside Marie, his mind was in one of those moments after climax when nothing else exists or matters in the world.

He fell asleep in the grass for a moment, and suddenly, the harsh real world again crashed in on him. It was the thunder of a new artillery barrage. Frank opened his eyes to find he was lying alone and naked on the riverside bank. There was no sign of Marie. He had no idea where she had gone; it was as if she had never been there.

Dressing and riding back to the Chateau, he found he had lost two hours.

"Where the hell have you been?" said his sergeant.

"Dirt in the carburettor again. I had to stop, strip the bloody thing down, and clean it," said Frank. The sergeant had little knowledge of engines, so Frank knew he would not question him.

That night, in his narrow bunk, he was unable to sleep. The endless pounding of the continuous heavy British artillery shelling of the German lines rang in his ears. Still, the scent of wood smoke also lingered in his hair.

Frank had signed up as a dispatch rider for one year or until the end of the war. His year was a few weeks from being completed when he killed a French deserter.

Many of these men roamed the countryside. Thousands had deserted after the Battle of Verdun. The war had turned some into savages who were becoming almost as dangerous to the Allied troops as the Germans. Returning from the frontline after eight hours on duty, Frank had been riding the old Triumph steadily down a dusty lane just one mile from his base. Only a hot meal and a night's rest were on his mind.

Without warning, three tramp-like figures dressed in the remains of blue uniforms jumped onto the lane just 100 yards ahead. Frank saw that at least one of them had a rifle, and it was pointing at him.

Skidding to a halt, he turned the Triumph through 180 degrees and twisted the throttle fully open.

Accelerating away, he felt a punch into his left shoulder; it spun him off the bike and onto the gravel of the lane. The poor Triumph continued riderless until it veered off the road and destroyed itself against a substantial elm tree.

Shaken but largely unhurt apart from his left shoulder, Frank looked up to see the four ragged men moving cautiously towards him. His right hand had already opened his holster, and his fingers gripped the pistol. When the armed and apparent leader of the group was no more than 10 yards from him, Frank drew his gun and fired. The shot hit the man in the middle of his forehead, and he dropped like a stone, face first, onto the gravel. Before Frank could fire another shot, the other three deserters fled into the trees.

Looking down at his shoulder, Frank could see that a bullet had gone straight through his arm. Surprisingly, there was little blood, and he was relieved to see that the bullet appeared to have missed any bones. He dragged himself up onto his feet and hobbled over to the dead French soldier lying face down on the lane. A trickle of bright red blood from the soldier's head formed a rivulet in the dry, grey dust. Frank turned the body over with his boot. He remained there for a few seconds before sinking down and sobbing at the side of the body. Before him, staring up with sightless eyes lay a young boy of no more than seventeen.

Doesn't even need to shave yet, thought Frank, as he gently closed the boy's eyes. Tears came as he sat in the middle of that dusty lane with the boy's head cradled in his lap. Frank's thoughts were of home.

He remembered watching his sister Joan sitting alone and silent for hours at the white, old pine table as she waited for news of their brother Joe and her beloved Norman. This boy's mother must be sitting in France waiting for news of her son. With his one good arm, Frank easily and quickly dragged the French boy's body to the side of the lane. It feels like a bag of bones, he thought.

He shuffled slowly, in mental and physical pain, back to the château. He could see why his brother had returned from this war destroyed. All this wasted life filled him with anger, but he was determined not to become a victim. If he survived, he was going to be happy and make a success of his life.

The injured arm ensured Frank's war was over. Within one month, he was shipped back to England. When he arrived home at the forge, he saw a tearful and emotional Joan, a smiling Joe, and an overexcited barking and jumping Spike. He even received a sullen "welcome home" from Jo.

Chapter Seven

Before the outbreak of the Great War, the Marshall family, like many others, lived a life untouched by the horrors of conflict. However, as the war unfolded, they were to experience more than their fair share of the sorrows it inflicted.

Just like for Frank, who was miles away in East Anglia, the start of the war had no real impact on George or the villagers of Sussex. George was quite happy at school, and although he wasn't outstanding at any subject, he was less lonely than at home. When he arrived home at the end of the spring term in 1916, he was surprised to find his father and mother present.

But Lord Marshall had not come home to see George. He was there to say farewell to Matthew and Stuart. The twins had recently joined the Royal Sussex Regiment as officers. The following day, they were leaving for France.

Dressed in his best formal clothes, George travelled in the Rolls Silver Cloud to the station with his parents to see his brothers board the train for France along with the rest of their regiment.

Victoria Marshall was distraught when the twins announced they were joining up. She had tried desperately to dissuade them, but it was futile. The weight of family honour and the pressure of the times made their recruitment inevitable.

George lined up with his parents as Stuart and Matthew formally shook hands with each of them. George thought how young and scared they looked. As his father shook their hands in turn, he said:

"Remember your crusader ancestors; don't let the family name down. Go out there and fight for your country." As George looked up at his mother, her face showed no emotion as she too shook her sons' hands. There were no embraces, no tears. The stark contrast with the emotional scenes of other mothers bidding their sons farewell was striking.

White steam filled the platform as the train slowly and noisily chugged away from the station. George felt momentary guilt that he was happy to see his brothers disappear into the distance. Still, like the train, the feeling soon disappeared.

Two months after his brothers had left for France, George was struggling through a Latin lesson when the headmaster walked into the classroom. He made his way directly to the teacher and whispered in his ear. Both men looked straight at George. The headmaster beckoned George to go with him. All the other boys watched silently as George slowly got up from his desk and followed the headmaster out of the room.

As they entered the headmaster's study, George noticed Matron Greaves was already there, sitting in a corner.

"George, please sit down," said the headmaster. "Would you like a glass of water?"

"No, thank you, sir," said George softly.

George had an idea about what was to come. One of his classmates had been summoned to the study two weeks earlier. In a low, grave voice, with a heavy heart, the headmaster delivered the devastating news to George.

"I regret to inform you, George, that both your brothers have fallen. They have made the ultimate sacrifice for the King, for England, and for Leamington School." George felt his legs fold under him as he collapsed onto the floor and whispered.

"What... Surely not both of them?"
"I'm afraid so. I've been told your brothers died together, fighting bravely for our country like so many of our other old boys." The headmaster's voice, though solemn, carried a note of pride for the fallen heroes.

Matron Greaves, her eyes filled with tears, helped George from the floor and guided him back to her room, where she made hot, sweet tea. The room was filled with a heavy silence, broken only by George's soft sobs. James arrived at the school in the Rolls a few hours later to take George home.

"Sorry to hear about your brothers, Master George," said James as he opened one of the passenger doors.

"Thank you, James," was all George could say as he stepped into the car.

Alone and silent in the back of the Rolls, with just his faithful Bertie for company, a single tear ran down his cheek again. Not in sorrow for his brothers, now he had recovered from the shock, whom he had never liked, but because this time he realised that his life had changed for good.

He was the only remaining son and now held full responsibility for the Marshall family's future. He knew his mother wouldn't let him forget that. He did have the wit to think; at least she would take some interest in my life now.

Matthew and Stuart Marshall were both killed on 18th July 1916. On this terrible day, the Royal Sussex Regiment lost 17 officers and 349 men. Stuart had watched with horror as his brother was blown apart in front of him, but without pause, he had continued his charge across the cratered wastelands until he was felled by machine gun fire from the German lines.

This tragic day would always be known as "The Day the Sussex Died".

Chapter Eight

A year after the war ended in rural Cambridgeshire, Frank had become successful at repairing the local bikes, motorbikes, and even a few cars that were starting to become more common on the village lanes and byways. With the business growing rapidly, he employed two young local lads to help.

His injured arm had now fully recovered. Frank had returned from the war as a hero but hated this glorification. The war had destroyed the lives of too many people he loved. When his war medals eventually arrived in the post, the British War Medal and Victory Medal were thrown to the back of a drawer in his workshop and forgotten. They were never to be displayed or talked about. The death and the horrors Frank had experienced in France would never leave him, and he saw no reason to be reminded of those terrible times.

New interests were gradually helping him get over those dark days.

Now nineteen years old, he had made his girlfriend Margaret Foster pregnant.
Margaret, the only daughter of village baker Reginald Foster, had always felt that she and Frank had been childhood sweethearts. Still, she had always been keener than Frank. Margaret would follow him and his mates everywhere as they grew up. Frank always tolerated her, but he had shown no genuine interest.

By seventeen, Margaret had bloomed into quite a pretty young woman. At five feet four inches tall, she was only four inches shorter than Frank. Margaret had light brown eyes the colour of ripe walnuts, dark-brown hair, freckles on her small, upturned nose, and a shapely figure.

Her mouth turned down slightly in the corners, which unfortunately made her appear rather unhappy, but this disappeared when she smiled.

Frank's war experiences undoubtedly caused him to grow up. Like many of his fellow survivors, he never talked in any detail about those experiences, but later in life, he would often think back and inwardly rage about the terrible and stupid waste of life that the war had caused.

Encouraged by Joan, who thought a girlfriend would help him settle down instead of roaring around on his motorbikes all the time, Frank started taking a serious interest in Margaret.

In the hot summer of 1919, early one evening after helping with the harvesting, Frank and Margaret found they were alone. They lay together in one of the haystacks they had just helped farmer Albert Betts build. The work had given them a real thirst, and they both managed to drink two large glasses of the homemade cider the farmer had given them.

Over the previous months, Frank often took Margaret to the Railway Arms for an evening drink. On the way back, they sometimes stopped in the playground of the village school they had both attended a few years earlier. The bench there was known as the "courting bench, " and they had tentatively been exploring each other's bodies. Now, as they lay hand in hand and giggled under the warm evening sun, Frank surprised himself and said,

"I love you, Margaret."

In response, Margaret smiled and said,

"Good, I love you too. It's time. I want to feel you inside me now Smiling at him, she sat up and unbuttoned her shirt, freeing her firm, round white breasts. Excitedly, Frank gently squeezed the right one before greedily taking the dark brown, stiffening nipple of the left breast into his mouth. Moaning, Margaret quickly pulled down Frank's shorts and underpants, releasing his rapidly stiffening cock. In one swift movement, she lifted her skirt and kicked off her knickers.

Grabbing his cock, she pulled him on top of her. Unfortunately, things were happening far too quickly for poor Frank. Still, as he tried to control himself, Margaret held him fast, parting her legs and stabbing him inside her.

This exquisite sensation was too much for Frank. He shuddered and came almost immediately. Embarrassed, he pulled out and away, quickly sitting up in the straw. Pulling bits of straw from his curly hair, Margaret, still giggling, said:

"Don't worry, Frank, you can practice every day when we are married."

Married! That word came as a real shock to Frank and sobered him up immediately. He certainly hadn't thought about marriage before.

Two months later, he had to. Margaret entered the forge while Frank kneeled, struggling to repair some bent forks on a customer's bicycle.

"Isn't it wonderful? I'm going to have your baby," she said, laughing. Margaret was both excited and delighted. All she'd ever wanted out of life was a husband and children.

Now, she was about to get both. A shocked Frank slowly put down the hammer he was holding. While still on his knees, he said,

"I expect we will have to get married then!"

"If that's your proposal, Frank Cartland, I accept." said a happy Margaret, "And I'll get Daddy to find us a house. Now, let's go and tell everyone."

In fact, Frank was not to upset about the prospect of marriage, as he desperately wanted to escape the depressive atmosphere at the forge. With an increasingly unpredictable John, a silent Joe and a religious, nervous Joan living there, he had started to dread going home each evening.

Frank had prayed earnestly before his father's death, but he didn't really have faith in any religion.

"How can there be a God?" he asked Joan.

"No God would allow the evil we have seen in this world."

Joan had no answers, but she needed to believe in something.

Frank also knew he needed much more space for his growing motorcycle business. He could see that marriage to Margaret, with her father's family money and help, would be an excellent opportunity for him.

Two weeks before the wedding, Frank, in a mild panic, said to Joan,

"I've got nothing to wear for the wedding, and I don't know anyone with a suit."

"Why don't you ask Doctor Jones? I'm sure he will have one," Joan replied

Frank went to see his friend and borrowed a brown suit. The only trouble was that it was about two sizes too large.

"It's going to look rather big on you," said Howard Jones, "but I'm sure Margaret won't mind." Meanwhile, Margaret's father indulged her. Her aunt made her wedding dress to the latest fashion pattern. It was cream with frills on the bodice, wide, puffy 'gigot sleeves', a long train, and a veiled hat. Her two little nieces, daughters of her brother Thomas, were to be the bridesmaids.

Frank wanted Joe to be his best man, but it was clear that Joe would not be able to manage the job. So, instead, he asked his old school friend, Fred Coles. Once again, the villagers walked up the hill to St Mary's church to celebrate rather than mourn. A mixed selection of guests gathered there. The few Cartland family members and Frank's friends did their best to fill the right-hand pews, while the left side were full in number and size. The majority of the three generations of the Foster family were bakers. They were round, loud, and jolly people.

It was a lovely autumn afternoon as Frank, with the organ starting "Here comes the bride", turned to watch a slightly plump Margaret happily walking down the aisle at her father's side.

The moment he said,

"I will" Frank, for an instant, thought, *what the hell am I doing here?*

Then, he was swept away by events, following the familiar rituals as if they were a dream.

After the guests had covered the couple in confetti, Margaret's cousin Sally caught the bouquet. Then the wedding party walked back down the hill. As they did so, the wind increased, wiping a shower of light brown leaves from the beech trees covering Frank and Margaret.

"Isn't it wonderful," said Margaret with her arm firmly around Frank's waist, "it's like walking through a golden snowstorm. This is the happiest day of my life." The reception was held in the Burlham village hall, with the Fosters providing a substantial wedding spread and a four-tier wedding cake. The Red Lion provided the casks of beer and cider. Unfortunately, as often happened, John's beer drinking was his downfall; by 8 pm, he had had far too much of it.

Margaret's cousin Sally had been sitting quietly on her own, resting after a few dances with her friends. In common with six of the other single women at the wedding, she had lost her sweetheart in the war. All weddings were now difficult to cope with, just a constant reminder of what she had lost. Now twenty-five, she was putting on a little weight but was still pretty and had not lost hope of finding a husband.

John, the beer giving him the courage he didn't usually possess, lurched across the room and sat beside her.

"You look lovely tonight, Miss Sally," he slurred.
"Will you come outside and give me a kiss?"
"No, I will not, John Cartland, please go away, you're drunk!" Sally replied.
"Why not? My stupid little brother is good enough for your cousin, so I should be good enough for you," said John loudly.

Reaching over, he tried to put his big hairy arm around Sally's shoulder. Sally's younger brother, Dick, having watched as John approached his sister, rushed across the room and grabbed John around the neck, pulling him onto the floor. It should have been an uneven fight as John was at least four inches taller and two stones heavier than Dick, but the surprise attack and too much drink took John off guard. Dick landed a punch square on John's chin, but the impact hurt his fist far more than it hurt John.

They continued throwing wild punches at each other, neither inflicting any real damage on the other, until they were eventually dragged apart, and the fight petered out. Slowly hauling himself up from the floor, John staggered outside and, to everyone's relief, didn't come back.

Joan went to a worried-looking Frank and said,

"I expect he will go home to his bed now. Don't let it spoil your big day."

The mood soon lightened, and everyone got back to enjoying the reception. Even Joan, who would usually go and make sure her 'boys' were all right, soon forgot about John. She was dancing and enjoying herself for the first time since the war.

Overall, it was a successful wedding day. A slightly merry Margaret continually told everyone that it was the happiest day of her life. The couple spent their first night together at The Rutland Arms in Newmarket, a wedding gift from Frank's uncle, Charlie Willes.
Frank made up for his lack of control two months earlier.

"Oh Frankie, you really are my man," sighed Margaret as they made love for the third time that night. The following day, at 9 am, after the happy couple had enjoyed a large breakfast of eggs, bacon and fried bread, Charlie Willes arrived with his pony and trap to transport them back to their new home, Ivy Cottage in Burlham.

The couple were a giggling, happy, carefree couple as they shook and bumped in the back of the trap. They had just three miles of happiness. When they arrived at the cottage, a nervous-looking Joan was waiting outside.

"I can't find John anywhere," she said, "and Sally hasn't been seen since she left the wedding reception to walk home last night. I'm worried sick."

"Have you been to look for him at the forge?" asked Charlie.

"No, I can't get in. The door is locked, and I can't find the key. I shouted through the door, but there was no answer," Joan replied.

"I expect he is inside sleeping off his hangover," said Frank. "I've got a spare key for the forge under my bed in the cottage; I'll get it."

They found it would only go some way into the keyhole when they tried the big key.

"It's locked from the inside, the key must still be in the lock," said Frank.

"We'll have to break the door down," said Charlie. "I'll get some help."

A few minutes later, Charlie came back with Constable Clarke, who had been riding by; also with them was Margaret's father, who had been on his way to greet the couple at their new home. By this time both Margaret and Joan were extremely distressed. They together sat together crying in the back of the trap.

Constable Clarke found a heavy sledgehammer, which he and Mr. Foster took turns to swing and slam into the heavy, black oak door. But the lock was doing its job too well and their efforts had little impact.

"We are going to need something much heavier to get through this bloody door," panted Charlie.

"Frank, run to Albert Betts and tell him we need to borrow his steam hammer."

Five minutes later, Frank came back with Albert. They were both struggling to carry the heavy instrument. A large crowd of villagers had gathered around to find out what all the noise was about.

"Go away, there's nothing to see here," Joan shouted at them, which of course made them even more curious.

Once enough pressure of steam had built up, Albert Betts directed the piston at the heavy door. Releasing the holding catch, the hammer thundered into it and the black wood splintered. With a sound disturbingly like a woman screaming, the great door gave way.

The site that greeted them was one Joan and Frank had seen before. This time it was their brother hanging from the great beam, not their father. Joan collapsed immediately. Margaret and some neighbours carried her back to the cottage. Frank, remembering scenes he had tried to shut out for years, just turned and ran away. He didn't stop until he reached the sloping banks of Devil's Dyke.

Tom Clarke, Charlie, and Albert Betts went inside the forge and shut out everyone else as best they could with the shattered door. Charlie found a big, old brown tarpaulin in the corner of the forge which he managed to hang over the lintel of the broken door. Between them they managed to untie the end of the rope and gently lower the lifeless body of John Cartland down onto the dirt floor of the forge.

"I'll go and get Doctor Jones," said Albert Betts, wanting a reason to escape the nightmare. On the workbench in the corner of the forge, Tom Clarke noticed a large poster advertising the funfair that had visited Burlham two weeks earlier. He walked over and picked it up. He was about to screw it up and throw it away when he noticed black smudge marks on his fingers. Turning the poster over he saw that the plain white back of the poster had writing on it in thick charcoal.

"Come over here, Charlie, and look at this," he said. With great difficulty they began to read.

It's me what done for them two old slags, the old man helped me get rid of the first un, but couldn't handle it an hung hisself. Now i gone too far, couldn't help meself when the urge comes cant control it didn't mean to kill poror Sally   just wanted her t love me. you all beter orf witd out me.

At the bottom was a sprawling signature, which could have read John Cartland.

Frank sat in his favourite spot high on the bank of the dyke under two gorse bushes. They always protected him from the worst of the wind, which often howled across the great green earthworks. This was the place he always came to when he needed to escape the bad times. Spike had followed him from the village and now sat panting at his side. From here they could see for miles. To his left, just one mile away, was the huddle of houses that was Burlham, with the top of the church towering above them. Sweeping his gaze right he saw the vast, flat fenlands, a straight line stretching away until it hit the large full stop that was the cathedral on the Isle of Ely. On a clear day he could make out its spires ten miles in the distance.

Frank suddenly realised that he hated John. Even though he had no knowledge of the note his brother had left, Frank felt sure he knew what his hanging body had meant, he must have hurt Sally.

He had never really hated anyone before, even his father who had beat him so badly. Frank felt that there was a good reason for all his anger.

He thought of poor Joan, whose whole life had been blighted by those around her. From the moment their mother died, Joan had been a victim of other people's actions. He knew today's events would finish her and he felt helpless to ease her pain.

Thankfully, Joe wouldn't be able to understand what was happening all around him. Frank rather envied his brother stuck in his own little world.

At least Edith had the good sense to get away from this cursed family, he thought.

As he sat on the bank, with the sun briefly coming out from behind the high clouds, once again, he decided that he would not be a victim, no matter what happened or what would happen next. He was determined to make a success of his life. Frank knew that there was a desire that had put a fire inside him and that nothing could put out his love for speed. Racing along the Cambridgeshire roads on the fine edge between disaster and glory was the only time when he felt utterly alive.

News of John Cartland's death had gone around the village like wildfire. With the arrival of the Inspector of Police from Cambridge, it wasn't long before the press started, once again, to descend like vultures on the unfortunate Cartland family. Sally's angry brother and father were soon at the remains of the forge door, demanding to know what had happened to their girl.

When they realised that Sally's body wasn't in the forge with John, they organised a search party. The scene was chaotic, with a couple of local police trying to keep control.

The crowd had rapidly become an angry mob that wanted some answers. If John Cartland hadn't already hanged himself, the mob would have done the job for him.

Just one day into her married life, Margaret was back at her family home, being comforted by her parents. The honeymoon was certainly over.

From his vantage point on the slopes of the dyke, Frank could see a line of people approaching. He walked down to meet them.

"What's going on?" he said to Margaret's brother, Dick, who was leading the train of locals.

"We are searching for my sister," Dick replied.

"We think your bastard brother has hurt or killed her; you Cartlands are all murderers."

Noticing Spike at Frank's side, he added,

"Even your bloody dog is a killer."

They all pushed past Frank, even his best man Fred Coles, almost knocking him over. Just twenty-four hours earlier, these same people had been shaking his hand and congratulating him; now, they spread out to start their search along the dyke.

As Frank watched the ragged line slowly disappear away from him he suddenly realised that Dick was right; he was a murderer, twice over. He was responsible for the deaths of the poor French soldier and his mother, who had died giving birth to him.

Head down, he and Spike started a slow, lonely walk back to Burlham to face the drama and sadness he knew he would find at the forge. The happiness and laughter of yesterday seemed like a lifetime ago. Arriving home, he pushed into the cottage through the growing crowds gathered outside. He sat at the kitchen table where his uncle and Doctor Jones were already seated. Joan and Joe had been given sedatives by Howard Jones and were lying in their beds.

"Sorry, Frank, it looks like your brother has hanged himself, and he's left a note," said his uncle sadly.

"What does it say?" asked Frank.

"John says he was responsible for both the old murders as well as for killing Sally," said Charlie.

"But that can't be true. They hanged the guy who killed the other two women, didn't they?"

"We all thought so, but it looks like John has confessed to those murders as well," Charlie explained.

This was far worse than Frank had expected. Not only had he lost a brother, but now the nightmare with the nation's press would start again.

With the Cartland family cottage once again under siege, Joan, Joe and Frank stayed together inside for two days. Joe, who didn't understand why all the noisy people were outside, became very agitated.

"I want them to all go away," he said. I want to take Spike for a walk. And why isn't John here?" He repeated the same questions almost every hour.

When Doctor Jones brought them the necessary supplies, he gave Joe more sedatives to ease his distress. Joan and Frank sat in silence for hours.

As they all expected, Inspector Davies arrived. Frank noticed that his hair and pencil-thin moustache had turned almost white since they had last met him before the war.

"We need to know if John had any special place where he may have gone last night," he said, looking directly at Frank.

"Don't know of any," Frank replied sullenly. "He spends, I mean used to spend, all his time either in the forge or down the pub."

"Well, if any of you think of anywhere, he might have been sure to let one of the constables know. I'm keeping two on duty outside to stop the press pestering you all."

"Thank you," said Joan dully.

For two days, from first light until darkness enveloped the countryside, a dozen policemen and most villagers continued their search for Sally, but no trace of her was found.

On the third morning, Constable Tom Clarke was cycling past the cricket field when he decided to stop and take another look. It was one of the likeliest places that John would have gone, but it had been searched on the first day. The pavilion had been built on the far side of the field, away from the road. It was only a simple three roomed hut with a home dressing room, an away team dressing room, and the main area where the scorers sat, and the teas served. When he entered, it was empty, as he had expected.

Walking outside, he went to the back of the pavilion and tripped over a wooden ladder lying in the long grass. *What do they need a ladder for down here?* He thought.

Then, looking up at the tiled roof, he noticed a small porthole window in the pitch of the building. Excited, he realized that there must be a room up there. He was dragging the ladder around to the pavilion's door when two local lads turned up.

'What are you doing with that ladder, Clarkie?" asked one of them.

"PC Clarke to you, cheeky little sod," he replied before adding, "Give me a hand with this; we need to find the trap door into the roof."

They discovered it above the door in the visitors' changing room. It was flush with the ceiling and almost unnoticeable.

Tom Clarke leant the ladder against the doorframe and went up. With difficulty, Tom pushed the hatch upward and poked his head through the gap. A dim light directed a beam from the east-facing porthole window. Highlighted on the floor of the loft lay Sally's body.

"Anything up there?" shouted one of the lads.

"Both of you run up to the village and get a message to Doctor Jones. Tell him we need him here urgently."

With the boys running off, Tom pulled himself into the loft and crawled across to Sally.

She lay, fully clothed, on her back and with her hands clasped together across her lap. Sally looked asleep, but he could see the ugly, purple bruises around her chalk-white neck.

The national press once again based themselves at the Red Lion pub and, much to the landlord's joy, drank the place dry. Reporters spent their time investigating all areas of the Cartland family, covering their pages with sensational, upsetting headlines. "Like Father like Son" was one of the most common.

No one seemed to bother much about the fact that poor Ralph Stock had been hanged for two murders that he hadn't committed.

The old Charlie Cartland suicide story had been dragged up again and given comprehensive coverage alongside that of his murderous son, John. The Cartlands were front-page news for a few days. Still, following the release of the confessions in John's suicide note and the discovery of Sally's body, there was little fresh news to report on. The press gradually drifted away and lost interest in the village of Burlham and the remains of the devastated Cartland family. They moved on to find fresh, new sensationalist stories.

All Margaret had ever wanted was an everyday family life, but it was a tough start to their marriage. Many of Margaret's relations wanted nothing to do with the Cartland family, and most of the villagers were, for a while at least, wary around Frank. *Surely, they can't really think I'm like him*. He thought to himself sadly.

With pressure from Margaret, they had persuaded her doting father to buy Ivy Cottage and its' orchards, which were just one hundred yards down the high street from the forge. Old Mrs. Grange had recently died at age 75, having lived in the cottage for 40 years, so the place was very run down.

The roof leaked due to broken and missing slates, and it really was Ivy Cottage, being covered in the invasive green plant. The clutch walls were crumbling and unstable in many places where the ivy roots had made their home. Frank didn't mind hard work. In fact, labouring all day helped to stop his worries, and he soon made the place habitable for his new family.

After three months of hard work, he started on his workshop when the house was fit for Margaret to move into. He wasted no time and soon built a large garage on the plot of ground next to the cottage. Already, Margaret could clearly see how her new husband's mind worked. "You have spent more time working on that garage than finishing the cottage, she protested.

"There's still lots more work to do in our home." But Frank was impatient. He was ready to expand his business. The new sign went up, again in golden yellow writing and with a dark green background, and Frank began trading as CARTLAND MOTORCYCLES.

The most challenging time came when he had to move all his bikes and equipment from the forge. It was the first time he had entered since John's death. He rushed in and pulled his bikes, engines, spare parts, and tools outside before slamming the repaired door shut with relief. The atmosphere inside the dark, old forge could only be described as menacing. Frank hoped he would never have to go in there again.

He felt very guilty as he packed up all his things, leaving Joan and Joe alone in the sad, quiet cottage, with only bad memories for company. Spike was putting on weight. He spent most of his days keeping Joe company rather than exercising outdoors, and it seemed that Joe had lost what little confidence he had built up prior to John's death.

Just seven months after Margaret and Frank's wedding, Margaret went into labour. When her waters broke and splashed on the kitchen floor, Frank was in his workshop across the yard. She staggered to the cottage door while screaming,

"Run to your grandmother's, Frank, and be quick." Agnes Willes, now 68, was still delivering to the Burlham children. It took just five minutes before she arrived at Ivy Cottage with a worried Frank at her side.

"Just stay out here, Frank," said Agnes as he tried to follow her inside the cottage. A nervous Frank lit another Woodbine and went back to his workshop.

He tried to finish rebuilding the engine he had been working on when Margaret had first screamed at him. He hammered and tapped as loud as he could to drown out the sounds of Margaret's pain coming from the cottage.

An hour later, his grandmother called out to him.

"You can come in now, Frank,". With relief, he dropped his spanner and ran into the cottage. In their bedroom, he saw a tired but smiling Margaret cradling their healthy baby girl in her arms. It was such a relief for him. Since his own birth had killed his mother, all childbirth filled him with dread.

"Can I hold her?" he asked.

"Of course, stupid, she's your daughter," said Margaret softly.

Taking the tiny bundle gently from her, he looked down at the shock of black curly hair and the round, pink face.

The baby's brown eyes were open and looking straight up at him. Frank suddenly understood that a fundamental change had occurred in his life; nothing would ever mean more to him than this tiny girl.

"Let's call her Mary, after my mother," he said, his voice breaking, as tears trickled down his cheeks.

Chapter Nine

Sexual experience for George had come much earlier than it had for Frank. Arriving home from school a day early for his summer holidays, in the carefree years before the war began, he had been excited as he rushed into the library. The latest copy of Autocar was in his hand. He intended to spend the afternoon absorbing the reports of the recent Tourist Trophy races on the Isle of Man and the latest Brooklands race meeting.

Upon opening the library door, he came face to face with Sarah, one of the kitchen maids. She was on her hands and knees and hard up behind her was his grunting, red-faced brother, Stuart.

For an instant George thought they were playing a game, but he soon realised what was really happening. He had watched the family prize bull servicing the heifers in the farmyard, and Sarah had the same blank, sad, and resigned look on her face as those cows.
George turned quickly and had his hand on the doorknob about to leave when Stuart noticed him and said,

"Hey, Georgie Porgy, don't go. Come over here, it's time you learnt how to do this."
Stuart made two hard thrusts into Sally and let out a low grunt. Slowly and reluctantly, George moved into the room and stood next to his elder brother.

"Now it's your turn, pull your trousers down and stand here," he said to George. Nervously George did as he was told. Unfortunately, although he felt some small stirrings in his little cock as Stuart roughly pushed him into Sally's hot, sticky backside, George was not ready for this experience. He stood shaking and unsure what to do next.

He was about to cry when someone said,

"Here, Georgie let me show you how it's done." It was his other brother Matthew. George hadn't noticed him sitting in an armchair watching him with amusement. "My Sarah needs a real man," he said, pushing George aside. He thrust himself into Sarah. George watched with a mixture of fascination and horror

"There!" Matthew exclaimed, "that's how to do it, Georgie." Finishing his violation he playfully slapped Sarah's pure white, round bottom.

"Thank you, Miss Sarah," he said. "Now get back to work." Sarah quickly straightened her skirts, stood up with difficulty and slowly walked to the door. She had not uttered a word.

The twins had walked out of the room laughing and joking soon after the poor maid. They left George alone within the walls of the dark, leather books, all thoughts of the *Autocar* forgotten. He still had his trousers around his ankles.

Six weeks later, the Marshalls were at dinner in the dining room at Sefton Manor. Lord John Marshall was sitting at the head of the large, dark oak table, and directly opposite him, Victoria Marshall sat with their twin boys.

Stuart was sitting on her left, and Matthew was on her right. James had already driven George back to school for the new term.

They had all finished their course of minestrone soup and sat in silence, waiting for the delivery of their roast beef. Suddenly, the door burst open, and a middle-aged woman rushed in carrying a large silver dish. With a triumphant flourish, she lifted the domed lid. A collective gasp rose from the family as they saw the dish full of steaming horse manure. Liz Porter was an assistant cook in the Marshall household.

Liz was also Sarah's mother, and before they had time to react, she had dumped great lumps of the brown horse shit into the laps of both boys. They yelled in surprised horror as stinking stains corrupted their neatly pressed trousers.

Turning to look straight at Victoria, she added, "Make sure you keep these chinless bastards away from my girl in future.

All this happened so quickly that initially none of the Marshalls had time to respond. Now Victoria came to her senses and shouted.

"Get this evil woman of here." She screamed. Her face the colour of beetroot.

The butler and two servants rushed in and grabbed Liz. Before she was dragged kicking from the room Liz shouted back,

"I see you all enjoyed the soup. You should, I poured the remains of my overnight chamber pot in it when cook wasn't looking."

Liz was crying as she shook off the hands holding her and, head held high, walked out of the room.

For minutes, the Marshalls sat in shocked silence among the mess. The quiet was eventually broken by the contents of Stuart's stomach splashing onto the stone dining room floor. No one had any appetite for roast beef. Victoria was next to make a sound. Her face crimson with rage and the bile rising in her throat.

"What have you two been doing to her girl?" she shouted at the, tearful, white-faced twins.

"Get upstairs and clean yourselves up."

"Quiet woman," boomed John Marshall. "Sounds like they have only done what the male Marshalls have done for generations - buggered the servants - it's what they are for!" He gave the boys a knowing wink.

Victoria stared at all three in turn and stood up with a look of total disgust on her face, sending her chair crashing to the floor.

"You all sicken me," she said and stormed out of the room. They were appropriate words as she rushed to the toilet.

George thought about that time in the library with Sarah many times over the following years. Later, after his brothers' deaths, he remembered that two other young girl servants, as well as Sarah, were no longer working in the kitchens.

"Where did the maid Sarah go?" he had asked James one day.

"She was sent away like all the other girls carrying your brothers' bastards," said James with considerable anger. George decided not to ask more questions.

The death of the Marshall twins had not been mourned by any of the Marshall servants. Most of the staff had lost good men from their own families in the war, and they certainly had no room in their broken hearts for those two boys.

With the death of her twins, Victoria Marshall focused her attention on her only remaining son, much to George's discomfort.

She had been utterly distraught at his brothers' deaths, but this was no ordinary mother's distress - she had invested twenty years of her life in their futures. That wasted time devastated her.

Initially, she had moved herself away to the South of France for eighteen months. Her parents' family owned a large, rambling villa just a mile outside Nice. It overlooked the Mediterranean Sea, and she retreated there, hoping it would help her recover.

At the end of the war, Victoria moved back to Sefton Manor. She aimed to turn George into the next Lord Marshall and ensure the family line continued.

With his mother away and his father absorbed in his own affairs in London, George found solace in his passion for driving. The exhilaration of his visit to Brooklands was etched into his memory, and driving the small cyclecar, painstakingly rebuilt by James, was a source of immense joy. In those moments, he was Charles Jarrott, his hero from Brooklands, racing around the farm fields. The thrill of pushing the limits, his heart racing with a mix of fun and fear.

James sometimes watched George driving from a distance. *He thought that boy will never be a successful racing driver. He is too afraid of hurting himself.*

Upon her return from France, Lady Marshall spent little time searching for a suitable wife for George. The Marshall family had a long-standing tradition of sending their sons to Trinity College, Oxford, for their education. The twins were destined to follow this path. With only George remaining, the pressure was on to secure the family's future through finding him a financially favourable marriage.

Victoria was quite happy to accept Leamington School's advice that George would not be suited to university life academically. She had other plans for him anyway. Apart from the need to ensure an heir, she had discovered that her husband had become an addictive gambler. He spent as much time at the Newmarket and Goodwood horse races as in the House of Lords, and his recent losses only added to their financial troubles. It was clear to Victoria that she was the only one who could secure the family's future.

Victoria was shocked when she arrived home from France to find their butler Sykes packing the family silver into a large box.

"Sykes, what do you think you are doing?" she asked.

"Lord John has instructed me to list and pack all this silver, my lady," he replied.

"We will see about that," she said and went to find her husband.

"What the hell are you doing with the silver," she demanded when she found her husband in the library.

"I've had a bad run on the horses lately. My luck will turn when I pay off my Bookmakers," he replied sharply.

Victoria realized that any protests from her would only provoke anger, so she remained silent and walked out. The experience left her determined that George would need to marry for money and a good family—and soon.

The family's financial situation was dire, with her husband's gambling debts piling up and the family silver being packed away. It was clear to Victoria that their only hope for a secure future lay in a strategic marriage for George.

.

Chapter Ten

"Fearless" Frank Cartland had, by 1921, become a successful motorcycle race rider. He had developed his riding skills around the fields and roads in the Fens and, of course, as a dispatch rider during the war. He started riding in trials events, but these were too slow for him, and he very soon progressed to motorcycle hill climbs and road races. He was given the nickname Fearless Frank due to his attitude to danger.

Having little money, Frank had no choice but to build his own motorbikes and engines. His success meant that other riders were soon keen to pay him to build their engines, too.

"Do you have to go away every weekend?" Margaret complained. "It would be nice if you could spend some time here with Mary and me for a change."

"I have to race myself to prove how good my engines are," replied Frank.

"But what you are doing is extremely dangerous. You have responsibilities now and a family that needs you here," Margaret tearfully said.

Following a recent race, Frank had made the mistake of telling Margaret that one of his fellow riders had been killed. He now needed the adrenaline rush that the race riding gave him; this had become the most important passion in his life. He knew Margaret was right, but rational thought would always come second when the alternative was speed and the thrill of racing.

Frank's continued success ensured that the motorcycle business was multiplying; he had doubled the size of his garage and workshop by building a new shed on the orchard. Driving around the country, Frank started to see car and motorcycle workshops with petrol pumps outside. *I need one of those*, he thought.

Frank went to see Fred Manchett, who had two pumps at his Cambridge workshop.

"How do I get one of these pumps for my garage, Fred"? Frank asked when he filled up his old van one day.

"I'll send the Shell rep over to see you," replied Fred.

By November 1922, Frank Cartland had the first petrol pump in any Cambridgeshire village. He was the proud owner of a slim yellow and red Shell pump capped with a lit white shell globe.

"You are just like a child with a new toy". Margaret had laughed as she watched him tenderly polish its' glass casing. Installing it had been backbreaking work. Joe and Spike tried to help dig the large pit needed to take the petrol storage tank, but they were usually in the way.

For a moment, having dug six feet down into the rock hard, chalky subsoil, and with his back aching and sweat pouring off him, Frank thought it would be good if John had been here to help. He hadn't thought about his dead brother in about a year.

In January of that year, Margaret discovered that she was pregnant again. She was delighted, Frank less so. Their first daughter, Mary, was a lively and healthy two-year-old.

From the moment she could walk, Mary would find her way into the garage and was happy to be at her father's side playing with bits of his old engines and his spanners. Her hands were always oily and mucky.

"Don't encourage her," Margaret would often say. "I want her to grow up like a normal girl, not a dirty mechanic like you."

The birth of Mary greatly affected Frank. Before her arrival, little had had any personal emotional impact on him, apart from the surreal excitement he always felt when racing on the edge between disaster and success.

But his feelings for Mary were different. His love for her was immediately strong—she was a part of him. Her happiness would always be the most important thing in his life, except when his racing passions got in the way.

Margaret was far from happy to witness Frank's continuing racing success.

"Even when you are here, you're not at home," she said when he returned after another weekend away. "You are always in that bloody garage."

Frank had won another race and was proudly carrying a new silver trophy, which interested her little. Margaret had always been a nervous girl, and now, as a woman with a family and the worry of Frank's racing, every little thing seemed to cause her concern. She just couldn't understand Frank's passion for danger.

"Why can't he be like normal men and just go to the pub, get drunk and play cricket?" She would often moan to Frank's sister. Joan could only agree with her. She couldn't understand her young brother either.

"I'm afraid he's always been like it," she told Margaret. "I don't think he will change now."

Those words were not the ones Margaret wanted to hear.

When Frank first started race riding, Margaret had supported his passion and had been happy to go with him to the race meetings. But with the early morning starts and the travel, often to bleak, cold, and wet places, the novelty soon wore off.

She was much happier staying at home with her family.

Their second daughter was born two weeks early, on a Saturday in September. Agnes Willes delivered her, as were all the other children in the village. The birth took place on another weekend that Frank was away racing.

They called their new daughter Emily. She was a sickly child and kept Margaret awake most nights, giving her one more thing to worry about. When he was home, Frank always seemed to be able to sleep amid any noise.

"If there was an earthquake, he wouldn't hear it," Margaret often complained.

Frank was spending much more time away from home. He was travelling all over England to race his beloved motorbikes.

His first visit to the Isle of Man TT races was in 1922 after he rebuilt an engine for one of his best customers, a local racer from Cambridge named Archie Jones.

"I've always wanted to race at the Isle of Man," Archie had said to Frank as he stood in Frank's workshop one day, watching him rebuild an engine. "And it just so happens that I have managed to get an entry this year. I want you to run the bike for me."

Frank didn't need any persuading to take Archie's AJS motorbike to the famous racetrack.

"I have to go and help him; it's my job, and he's paying me," Frank said to Margaret, angry, when he told her he would be away for a week.

"Don't be surprised if I'm not here when you return," Margaret replied. "The girls and I are going to stay with my parents."

Frank knew the Foster family would welcome their daughter and grandchildren with open arms so that threat didn't worry him. Reginald Foster had never understood Frank. He offered Frank the chance to join the family bakery business soon after the marriage and he was shocked by Frank's answer.

"Thanks, Mr. Foster (Frank never managed to call him Reginald), but I will build my motoring business. I can't imagine being a baker."

Frank and Archie happily set off early one misty June morning on the long road trip to Liverpool.

Standing at the front of the ferry as it slowly entered Douglas Harbour, Frank could feel the excitement building inside him. The buzz of excitement building from the hundreds of like-minded motorcycles that now surrounded him forced him to shiver.

One visit to the island, and he was hooked. He became determined to race at the Isle of Man in 1923. They had all travelled there for one reason: to ride their motorbikes around this dangerous, challenging course as fast as possible.

Before the trial laps, Frank could see Archie Jones was highly nervous. He spent more time in the latrines than the pits. Cautiously, Archie went out on his first lap. Still, unfortunately, he was utterly overwhelmed by his experience of the Isle of Man course. Much to Frank's disgust, Archie entered the pits after only three slow practice laps. White-faced, he took off his helmet.

"Sorry, Frank. I think there's something wrong with the engine; it doesn't have much power."

"Alright, I'll look at it," said Frank without much enthusiasm.

What Frank really thought was ... *the old bugger had scared himself silly.*

This was, in fact, the truth. Towards the end of the third lap, Archie had grown in confidence before arriving at Governor's Bridge quickly. The AJS had leapt into the air, and that split second of terror would live with Archie forever. He thought he would die, but he managed to keep control of the bucking bike and ride slowly back to the pits.

The pit area next to Frank and Archie was occupied by a natural extrovert, a little guy called Freddie O'Hare.

Frank had been watching him all morning with great interest. Freddie was already well-known as a rapid motorcycle rider. He was always busy and covered in grease as he swore and worked all hours on his bikes.

He had a cigarette permanently clamped between his teeth, and when he jumped on his motorbike, he drove like the wind.

He's like an angry little wasp, thought Frank. This was just the sort of guy he could relate to.

Freddie was seven years older than Frank and already a very experienced TT rider. He first raced on the Isle of Man in 1912.

When Archie went off to change out of his leathers and revisit the restrooms, Frank boldly approached Freddie, who had just removed the carburettor from his bike.

"Would you mind trying out this AJS for me, Mr. O'Hare?" said Frank.

"I'd really like to know what you think about my engine. The rider thinks it's no good."

Freddie looked up from his bike and, upon seeing the curly-haired, nervous-looking young man standing next to him, said,

"What's your name, lad?"

"I... I'm Frank Cartland. It's my first time at the Isle of Man."

"Sure, I'd be happy to try the bike, Frank. Let me finish putting the carb back on this piece of shit first."

"I ... I thought you did a fast time this morning," said Frank, slightly surprised. "Yeah, but I had to nearly bloody kill myself to do it. Herbert told me this engine would be one of his best, but it only got power at the top end of the rev range. It's bloody near impossible to drive around this hell hole." Frank knew that Herbert Wilson had been one of the top motorbike engine builders for the past five years and that his engines had won five TT races.

Frank wishes he hadn't asked Freddie to try his engine at that moment.

Strapping on his helmet and pulling down his goggles, Freddie jumped on the AJS and roared off. Archie returned to the pits just in time to see his motorbike disappear up the road in a cloud of grey dust.

"Hey, who the Hell's gone off on my bike?" he shouted to Frank.

"Ah ... that's Freddie O'Hare. He asked if he could try out the bike, he's thinking of getting an AJS," Frank lied.

"Oh, I suppose that's all right then," Archie said. Freddie was his hero.

Three laps later, after lapping fast, almost as quickly as on his bike, Freddie returned to the pits.

"The bike's crap, but the engine is fucking marvellous," said a grinning Freddie as he pulled down his goggles.

"Frank, my boy, you can build a new engine for me anytime," he said, putting a greasy arm around Frank's shoulder. After hearing Freddie's comments, a despondent Archie Jones said,

"Ok, that's it for me, Frank. I'm not up to racing. I'm retiring today, and from now on, you can race my bike."

From that day forward, Freddie and Frank became firm friends. Freddie saw in Frank a reflection of his younger self. Both men had left school early, without much education, had come from working-class families, and had started rebuilding bicycles before progressing to motorcycles. Freddie could see the same obsessive passion he felt for racing reflected in young Frank's eyes. Frank's engine-building reputation grew rapidly for the next three racing seasons. Once Freddie O'Hare started winning races using Frank's engines, many more racers knocked at Frank's workshop door. They were prepared to pay a high price for a Cartland-tuned engine.

The once peaceful, sleepy village of Burlham now often resounded to the sounds of high-revving motorcycles, upsetting the old locals and drowning out the birdsong.

The Cartland motorcycle business was expanding fast.

Chapter Eleven

Frank's first visit to the famous Brooklands track in Surrey was in 1923 when he raced alongside Freddie O'Hare. Frank was riding the AJS that still belonged to Archie Jones.

The scale of the place shocked him. Instead of the narrow roads, he was used to racing along, Brooklands was a new world. Emerging from the tunnel under the track, Frank suddenly found himself in a vast amphitheatre, with the enormous width of the high banking filling his vision. His senses were hit by a strong scent of pine from the forest of trees on the banked area to his right. Then suddenly came the additional and familiar, intense smell, his favourite … the fumes of Castrol R drifting up from the paddock.

Venturing out onto the dirty-white concrete track, Frank quickly found that his bike wasn't suited to the high, bumpy banking. However, his bravery ensured they were the tenth quickest after the practice period.

Forty noisy and smoky bikes roared out from the start in front of the Vickers sheds. Holding his tenth place for two laps, Frank had the twist grip throttle wide open when the AJS broke its chassis halfway around the Byfleet Banking. Fortunately, although it gave Frank a bit of a scare, he brought the sparking bike to a safe stop, its chassis scraping the floor.

Racing on the fast Brooklands track had been Frank's new, exciting, overwhelming experience.

"I just held the throttle wide open and turned into the Byfleet Banking. The AJS powered halfway up the slope, and we just sat there, all the way around flat out," he said excitedly to Archie Jones as they pushed the broken bike back into the paddock.

Archie just said.

"Rather you than me".

Like George Marshall many years earlier, Frank had fallen in love with the Brooklands experience.

He excitedly explained this to Howard Jones when he got back home.

"It's a complete contrast to the Isle of Man, but if you love speed, it's brilliant," he said. "The wide track and open banked turns suck you in, and it makes you want to go faster and faster with every lap."

Overhearing this conversation from the next room, Margaret ground her teeth together. She had grown to hate the racing season. Between April and October, Frank was away from home almost every weekend, and she was never sure he would be coming back each time he left.

"Good of you to grace us with your presence," she would say on the odd weekend he was home.

Much to her dismay and Frank's delight, their daughter Mary continued her interest in engines in preference to dolls. She had become a real tomboy. Whenever Frank left for a race, there were tears and tantrums.

"Take me with you, take me with you," Mary would say, clinging to his leg.

At 5am one July morning, Frank and his mechanic Pete were ready to leave for a race meeting. Frank was surprised there was no sign of Mary; he had expected the normal tears and protests at being left behind. Slightly disappointed, Frank thought she must have stayed in bed this morning. He decided to look in and give her a kiss goodbye. But Mary was not in her bedroom. In some panic now, Frank rushed to wake up Margaret.

"Mary's not in her bed; I can't find her," he said.

Growing frantic, with Margaret almost hysterical, they searched the house, the workshop, and the garden sheds. Then Frank had an idea. He opened the van's back doors where the motorbike and all the tools were securely stored away. Just as he thought, there was an extra passenger. Mary had taken blankets and a pillow from the house and made a cosy den for herself next to the bike.

"Come out of there this instant," shouted Margaret, angry and relieved.

Frank reached in and lifted his sobbing little girl out. Carrying her back to her bed, he tucked her in and whispered in her ear,

"Promise I'll take you next time."

Frank started taking Mary to some local race events. He thought she would soon lose interest, but her interest just grew stronger. Hence, Frank built her a little motorised bike.

"Not content with killing yourself, now you're going to kill my daughter," said an angry Margaret when she saw the machine.

"It will only go at 5mph, so she can't hurt herself," said Frank, once again trying to justify his actions to his hostile wife. Mary was delighted with her new toy. "Oh, thank you, Daddy," she squealed, "now I'm going to be a racer just like you." Her mother rolled her eyes and turned away, feeling helpless. Mary was soon chugging around the village, upsetting the elderly locals, just as her father had done years earlier.

Frank had become obsessed with winning an Isle of Man TT race. He couldn't afford to race there until 1925, and then it was on an old bike belonging to Freddie O'Hare. Frank entered it for the Junior TT. Freddie had used the bike the previous year to win the race, but the bike was now a year old. With the rapid development of fresh machines, his bike needed to be updated, and Frank struggled to keep up with the newer bikes. After practice, he was despondent to be only the fifteenth quickest.

"Cheer up, Frank," Freddie said. "I'll take you for a drink tonight; that'll take your mind off it."

Then, thanks to Freddie, Frank was introduced to some of the other pleasures the Isle of Man offered the riders. Each year, Freddie stayed at the Metropole Hotel in Ramsey. The hotel manager reserved a room for him. It was room 8 - his lucky number. There were several girls on the island who "collected" famous riders. Still, Freddie had had a regular partner, Hazel Compton, for a few years. She would always spend the nights of TT week with Freddie and be in the winner's circle, waiting to share his glory and champagne after the race.

Before practice in 1925, Freddie had introduced Frank to Hazel. Is he going to be as famous as you?" Hazel asked Freddie after Frank had gone off to work on his bike. "If he is, my friend Susan would like to meet him."

"Of course, he bloody is he's a quick lad," said Freddie.

"Let's fix them up for tonight," came the reply. Frank found himself at dinner sitting opposite a pretty, freckled brunette called Susan Nolan that evening. When Freddie had told him earlier that evening that he had someone he wanted Frank to meet, Frank had assumed it would be another racing guy. He certainly wasn't expecting this attractive young woman that he now had sitting opposite him. After a few too many beers, they were all in a very relaxed mood.

Walking back along the seafront, Susan put her arm around Frank, who instinctively bent down and kissed her.

"Are we going back to your room?" asked Susan.

"Looks like we are," Frank replied smiling.
Freddie had booked Frank into the Metropole in the room next to him. Frank soon found that Susan was a very willing and experienced partner. The hotel walls were thin, and they could hear the moans and creaking beds from Freddie and Hazel's activity next door.

This made them even more aroused. Frank did not get off to sleep until 3 am.
He had asked for an alarm call at 6 am, and when it came, he felt terrible. He had a splitting headache and knew he had to be ready to start the race at 9 am. He was not at all happy.

Beside him, Susan was sobbing.

"What's the matter with you?" said Frank. "Are you sorry you stayed?"

"No... it's not that," she said, sniffing. "I'm just worried about what will happen to you today."

"I'll be fine," said Frank, "why would you worry about me?"

"Well, last year, I spent the night in this same room with Johnny Halliday, and he was killed the next day. And the year before Robert ..."

"Get dressed and bugger off out of here," a terribly angry Frank interrupted. The scar on his forehead was glowing pink.

Crying, Susan gathered up her clothes and did just that.

Unlike most of his racing mates, Frank rarely swore. But now he was mad and upset, not with that stupid girl, but with himself. Frank had let himself down.

He had come to the Isle of Man to race his bike, not to sleep with a local good-time girl. *I've let my cock rule my head again*, he thought.

The race didn't prove a success for Frank. Although he finished without actual incident, he was in tenth place. He knew he had been too careful and too slow. He swore he wouldn't let it happen again. In future years, he wouldn't drink before a race and always ensure that he slept alone.

Frank had decided not to race at all in 1926. He was determined to save all his money to afford a motorbike good enough to win the Isle of Man Senior TT in 1927. When he told Margaret he wouldn't be racing the following year, she didn't give him a chance to explain his reason.

"Good, it's about time you grew up and stopped playing these stupid, dangerous games," she said. "You will have plenty to do here; the house needs painting, the fence is falling, and the trees in the orchard need pruning, just for a start. Then you can spend some weekend with me and the girls for a change."

Once again, things did not all turn out as Margaret had hoped. Frank was busy building engines and looking after his racing customers, so he was still away many weekends. Also, because of Freddie O'Hare, he did manage to visit a racetrack that he had been avidly reading about in his motoring magazines. It would make a lasting impression on him. Spa-Francorchamps in Belgium was the circuit.

"Frank, I really could do with your bloody help next week," Freddie had said when he called at the garage. He had arrived to pick up the new engine Frank had just finished building for Freddie's TT Norton motorbike.

"I'm racing my sidecar outfit next weekend, and my stupid passenger has broken his bloody leg. Would you do me a favour and stand in for him?" "Sure thing, course I will," said Frank without a second thought.

"Great. I'll pick you up on Tuesday morning at about 6. We're catching the lunchtime ferry from Felixstowe."

"Felixstowe?" said Frank. "Where are we going?"

"Spa, of course," said Freddie as he jumped into his Austin van. "Make sure you bring your passport," he shouted out the window as he left.

"What do you mean you're going to Belgium next week?" said a seething, Margaret. "I told the girls we would take them to the seaside at Clacton."

"Sorry, but I can't let Freddie down; he needs me," said Frank weakly. It was a rather unfortunate response.

Now, almost screaming at him, Margaret said,

"I really don't understand you, you bloody stupid fool. You can let your family down, but not that horrible little man."

The strained atmosphere in the Cartland household was made even worse on Sunday. Charlie Willis called in to see them for a cup of tea.

"I hear you are off to Belgium next week, Frank," he said. Charlie had been horse racing in Belgium many times and had ridden many winners before the war.

"Belgium's a great country; you'll love it," Charlie continued. "The locals are all great company. I'll give you the address of a friend in Brussels."

Frank gave him a quick kick under the table to shut him up. Margaret sat stony-faced and silent.

On Monday evening, Margaret returned with their girls to her parents' bakery again. Without saying goodbye, she left him alone in Ivy Cottage. It was with considerable relief that Frank got into Freddie's van early on Tuesday morning.

Together, they trundled happily off to Felixstowe. His family problems were soon left behind and forgotten.

Thankfully, the ferry crossing was smooth, and by late afternoon, they were driving on the long, straight road leading to Brussels.

It was almost dark when Freddie said,
"Let's stop here for the night."

They could see the lights of a village ahead. Outside, there was a small building with a petrol pump that looked remarkably like Frank's garage. As they stopped the van outside the garage, a skinny young lad came to meet them.

"DO YOU SPEAK ENGLISH?" said Freddie in a slow and loud voice.

"No need to shout at the poor boy," Frank said. He was about to try some of his pidgin French.
The lad continued.

"Oui ... I do ... petit ... a little, me Robart Virrea, welcome to our home...Mr. O'Hare."

"Could we stay here tonight?" said Frank. With the help of hand signs, they made the lad understand, and they were invited into his home. Inside, his father greeted them like long-lost brothers, shaking hands and hugging both.

Robart had disappeared into another room. He returned with a pile of motorcycle magazines, proudly opening one to show a grainy picture of Freddie. He was in his oily overalls, had a fag in his mouth, and was carrying the TT Silver Trophy.

"Please, Mr. O'Hare, will you sign for me?" said Robart. Freddie, of course, was delighted to be the centre of attention. After a large breakfast, they filled the van with fuel from the garage pump and continued their merry way to the Spa the following day.

They had arrived at Spa before they realized it. Driving onto the road at La Source hairpin and down the hill, they suddenly found they were already on the race circuit.

Leaving the trailer and bike in the paddock with some other recently arrived English riders, Freddie and Frank went for a drive around the 14km circuit. It was only a short time before they understood what a high-speed and dangerous track Spa Francorchamps was.

"Bugger me, it's going to be flat out for most of the lap," said Freddie.

"It's so narrow that you can reach out and touch the houses and trees," said a slightly worried Frank. "For Christ's sake, don't do that," said
Freddie. "You won't have much to do. Just lean right over the back of the bike at the three hairpins, and the rest of the time, just stay flat down in the sidecar out of the air stream."

Frank looked doubtful.

After their new Brussels friends had given them a bed the previous night, the pair spent the following night sleeping in the back of the van. Frank didn't sleep much. For the first time in his life, he felt slightly scared. Practice day went well. Freddie rode sensibly as he learned his way around the long track. Although not entirely happy having someone else in control of his destiny, Frank started to enjoy the experience.

He quickly learned how to move around the sidecar to balance the bike on the corners and bends. Freddie was the one person he trusted with his life. As practice ended, they were fifth fastest and quite satisfied with their efforts.

They enjoyed a few beers that evening in the bar of Le Relais de Pommard, a hotel next to the circuit. Two other English riders were there, Jimmy Smart and his sidecar passenger, Peter Houge. They had qualified third in the practice session.

This pair had been the most successful British sidecar partnership for the past three seasons, and they had won the Isle of Man sidecar TT the previous year. "Better watch your bloody back tomorrow, Jimmy, I'll be coming for you in the race," joked Freddie.

"You won't see me for dust, old mate," said Jimmy. Have another beer and shut up."

Peter had been Jimmy's sidecar passenger for the last four seasons, and Frank was keen to get some tips about how to balance the bike through the frighteningly fast Masta Kink.

"I almost smashed my head against the house on the left there this morning," said Frank.

"Yeah, it's pretty hairy, isn't it? We're doing a ton through there. Keep your head down," said a sullen Peter. "Thanks, but I'd already decided to do that," said Frank sarcastically.

126

"Sorry, Frank, but I cannot say much more. It's just instinct, really. Follow the bends and lean into them. You're like me here because you need the buzz." After a short pause, he added.

"Sometimes I wish I didn't. This place scares me."

"Me too," said Frank. "I'll get you another drink." Like Frank, Peter had a wife and two young children in England.

"I've decided this will be my last race," he said. "My wife's been nagging me to stop... I'll be thirty-five next week. The kids are eight and ten, and I've not seen much of them growing up over the past four years. I've been lucky so far, but I'm going to pack this mad game in. Haven't told Jimmy yet so please keep it to yourself."

"Course I will," said Frank.

Both remained silent and sipped their drinks, thinking about the risks they would face in the morning. Race day dawned overcast and cool, but this Ardennes region's weather was always highly unpredictable.

The sidecar race was run over ten laps and began in dry conditions at one p.m. Two races for singles had already been held: a senior 350cc and a Junior 250cc.

The atmosphere was tense before the start of the sidecar race. A popular local Belgian rider had gone off the road on the straight before Stavelot when his engine had sized. News that he had been killed came through to the paddock just as the sidecar outfits were preparing to go out for their race.

The conflicting emotions running through Frank's head were extreme. He was looking forward to the challenge of this great track, but he knew his future remained in the hands of Freddie, who was already fired up for the race. Frank didn't like this feeling of not being in control.

"Okay, Fearless, let's bloody do this. See you on the other side," Freddie said, shaking Frank's hand.

Frank's mouth was dry, but he managed to say: "Yeah ... let's do it."

At that moment, he wished he were back home or anywhere else. They strapped on their helmets and pulled down their goggles.

Twenty sidecar outfits were on the grid. The pervasive noise smells, and smoke invaded Frank's senses as the engine revs rose to a crescendo.

All the riders were straining, holding the engines against the brakes, until the drop of the Belgium flag released the mass of screaming, swarming, swerving sidecars.

The race started well for them. By lap four of the ten-lap race, Freddie's Douglas bike was going well in a comfortable fourth place, only six seconds behind Jimmy and Peter.

Freddie became more confident with each lap. Now flat out through the daunting Masta Kink, Frank became aware he was smiling. Much to his surprise, he was enjoying himself.

They were closing the gap to Jimmy, and as they came down the hill and passed the pits to start their final lap, Frank could clearly see his HRD outfit. It was only two seconds ahead at the 11 km point of the lap, and they were gaining with every yard. Frank edged Freddie on. As they approached the fast left-hand bend at Blanchimont, Frank noticed Peter glance back and urgently give a slowdown signal. Freddie instantly relaxed his throttle hand, and the bike slowed, but they were still travelling fast as they rounded the bend to find that the track was soaking wet.

A sudden localized shower had rendered the track glass-like. The Douglas slid sideways as Freddie frantically fought for control. Frank instinctively moved his weight over the sliding rear wheel, and somehow, Freddie managed to keep the unit on the road. In a flash, they were through and continued quickly down through the left-hand curve and onto the La Source hairpin. Accelerating out of La Source, they were greeted by the chequered flag to end the race.

Most parts of the Spa circuit were still dry as they went out on their slowing-down lap. Freddie grinned at Frank and slapped him on the shoulder. Frank grinned back and gave him the thumbs-up sign. Both were happy to have finished in a good position, although they were unsure what that position was.

When they reached the Blanchimont turn, it had stopped raining, and a weak yellow sun appeared. The low, grey clouds cast faint, long shadows on the people and the ambulance, which was blocking the track.

"Stop the bike, Freddie. Let's find out what's happened," shouted Frank.

Freddie slid the Douglas to a stop. They left their bike and ran to the edge of the track. Here, a six-foot-high thorn hedge bordered a ten-foot-wide strip of grass. Frank's nose picked up his favorited smell of fresh-cut grass. Then he noticed the deep grooves in the grass leading to a large hole in the hedge.

"I don't like the look of this," said Freddie as they walked towards the hole. Looking over the hedge, Frank replied,

"Christ! There's a twenty-foot drop through here."

They could see a group of people gathered below them around the twisted remains of Jimmy Smart's HRD motorbike. Frank could just make out the number nine - Jimmy's lucky number. Others were lifting a lifeless body onto a stretcher.

"Look...over there, it's Jimmy," said Freddie, pointing to the left. They watched their friend hobbling slowly away from the scene.

"Then that must be Peter on the stretcher," said Frank quietly.

They walked back to the Douglas, and Freddie automatically drove back to the pits. The news from the deeply distressed Jimmy was the worst.

"There was no warning," he explained. "One second it was dry, next the track was like a skating rink ... there was nothing I could do."

Jimmy and Peter had been thrown in different directions when the bike had gone through the hedge and hurled down the drop. Jimmy was the lucky one, bouncing across the moss and pine floor, somehow missing all the fir trees. The soft moss had cushioned his fall, and with relief, he got up. He was bruised but largely uninjured. Dusting himself down, he went to find Peter. Jimmy saw him lying face down in the Eau Rouge stream, which ran alongside and under the Spa circuit.

"There was no blood, nothing. I...I thought he had just been knocked out. Then, when I pulled him out, his neck ..." Jimmy broke down completely. It was evident that Peter's luck had finally run out.

His descent had been abruptly halted as his body slammed into the large trunk of a Belgian fir tree. Death was instant, his neck broken.

There were no celebrations that evening at Spa. The third-place trophies Freddie and Frank had won were discarded in the van's back. Arrangements had to be made for Peter's body to be returned to England. Frank and Freddie stayed on to help Jimmy with the harrowing task. Frank had sent a telegram home to let the family know he was okay but needed to stay in Belgium an extra day. He didn't give a reason.

The following afternoon, the body of Peter Hough was given a sombre civic send-off from Spa station. His flower-bedecked coffin was placed on the 3pm train to begin his last long journey back home to Manchester. As they watched the steam train move slowly out of Spa station, Frank said,

"You realise the last thing Peter did was warn us?"

"Yeah, I know, bloody good bloke," said Freddie. Freddie and Frank spent most of their trip home in silence. They didn't stop at Brussels as planned, as they were impatient to catch the next ferry. Both were reflecting on the events at Spa. Freddie broke the silence. "Fucking place," he said. "I'm never going to race there again."

Frank said nothing. He had been thinking just how much he had enjoyed the race until that fatal moment. Now, he felt guilty. He knew that despite Peter's death, he would go back and race at Spa if he ever had the chance.

He also knew that Freddie would too. This guy had won races at the most dangerous track in the world, the Isle of Man. With his nature, Freddie would soon recover from this shock and look forward to his next trip to Spa Francorchamps.

When he got home, Frank said little of his Belgium trip. He was trying to keep Peter Hough's death from his family. Unfortunately, the motorcycle press called to interview him on the Wednesday after the event. Hence, Margaret and Joan soon found out.

"That could have been you, riding with that madman O'Hare," Margaret shouted at him.

"Well, that was my first and last sidecar race," said Frank, and he meant it. He really had no intention of repeating the experience. From now on, he will control his fate when he races.

The following month, he went to the Isle of Man to look after Freddie O'Hare's motorbike. However, he was still determined to race there the following year.

Chapter Twelve

For the 1927 race, Frank had spent all his and his family's money, amounting to £95, on a new Norton racing motorbike. When she found out, Margaret's distress was evident.

"How could you be so irresponsible?" she complained when he turned up with the gleaming new, black racing motorbike. "You have a family to support." With the silver and black petrol tank proudly displaying the Norton name on both sides, Frank had been excited and keen to show off his new pride and joy. Now, he had to defend himself once again.

"It will be worth it when I win," he said, trying to justify the cost to himself as much as to Margaret. "We will get even more customers, and I will be able to sell the Norton for a profit."

"We never see you now as it is, so how will more customers help that? You're a selfish bastard," she said before storming out of the workshop and slamming the door.

Frank hadn't had time to answer. He was angry. *Why does this woman always make me feel so guilty?* he asked himself. *She tries to take away all my pleasure.* The Norton CS1 bike, with its single-cylinder overhead cam engine, was a new design developed especially for the 1927 TT races.

This bike is the most beautiful thing I've seen since the old Triumph that Howard Jones arrived on back in 1913, he thought with a grin.

Frank and Peter Betts left Burlham at 4 am that June morning, once again starting the long journey north for Liverpool, where the ferry that would take them to the Isle of Man where fate waited. Frank was full of confidence and happiness as he steadily drove the Morris van, with the Norton carefully strapped into the space behind him and his young mechanic Pete at his side. This was going to be his year. Mary had woken up to give him a good luck kiss.

"I know you will win, Daddy. I will pray for you at church on Sunday". She'd whispered.
Margaret had stayed in bed, pretending to sleep. She wouldn't even say goodbye.

Once more, Frank stood at the front of the old ferry, watching as the captain slowly maneuvered the ship into the dock at Douglas Harbour. Frank knew the next few days would be the most important of his life.

The Senior Tourist Trophy was the most prestigious motorcycle race of the season. All the top riders from the UK, Europe, and even two from Australia had travelled to the Isle of Man to win it. At 7 am on a misty Tuesday morning, each rider presented themselves and their bikes for scrutiny. Frank was allocated the number 51 for the event. With shock, he remembered that his father had been 51 when he died. It was the day

Frank's real life had begun. He felt that must be a good omen.

Practice started the following morning, June 15th, at 6 am. The day dawned dry and cool, with a light mist over the mountain section of the course. The Isle of Man roads were still open to regular traffic for practice. One of Frank's rivals, Archie Wright, also riding a new Norton, approached Kirk Michael extremely fast and was forced to brake hard to avoid a local delivery van moving slowly in the middle of the road. Archie lost control of the bike and was thrown off, sliding headfirst into a flint wall. The undamaged bike slid down the road. Archie was killed instantly, his neck broken on impact with the solid wall.

Frank arrived on the scene only twenty seconds after the accident and clearly saw Archie's broken body as he slowly rode past. He immediately closed his mind and focused on the narrow road ahead.

Then he remembered what Freddie had once said to him. *"When I see something bad, I twist the throttle wide open and go as fast as possible. Because I know most other guys slow down when they see a bad accident."*

At the time, Frank thought that was wrong and uncaring. Now, he realised that winning was all that mattered to him and at any cost.

Every rider knew that death at the Isle of Man was part of the significant risk. Each time they ventured out onto the 37 miles of public roads that made up the course, there was a chance they would never come back.

Some of the hazards they faced were narrow roads, stone walls, lampposts, and a steep drop off the side of the mountain sections.

It was an accepted part of the "ride for glory" for these men, who were only alive when risking all. Frank was happy with the sleek black Norton. Without taking too many risks, he managed third fastest in practice. It was his first ride on the bike, and he was quicker than his great-mate, Freddie O'Hare, who was riding an HRD machine for the 1927 race.

The commentators made a big thing of the rivalry between them.

"Here come Flying Freddie and Fearless Frank. Who will be the quickest on this lap?" became a standard announcement.

"Bloody hell, Fearless, it looks like I'm going to have to get my finger out to beat you this year," Freddie said to Frank after practice.

"It's time you made way for us youngsters," Frank joked, knowing Freddie was becoming sensitive about his age.

Frank slept well the night before the race, and he was optimistic when the start time arrived. Confident that he could win the famous silver trophy, he knew he could ride some corners faster than he had in practice.

Frank's start time approached. He pulled on his brown leather helmet and adjusted his goggles. "Good luck, Frank," his mechanic Pete said as he slapped him on the back.

Now, he was utterly alone. He stood in silence, waiting, his hands tightly clutching the black rubber grips on the drop handlebars of his precious Norton. Looking forward at the vast expanse of empty road ahead of him, he was calm, and his mind was clear. He was ready. With a stopwatch in hand, the starter raised and then dropped his flag. At last! Frank accelerated away on the most important ride of his life.

The Senior TT covered seven laps of the 37-mile course. By lap 5, after racing for more than three hours, Frank stormed into his pit for his last petrol refuelling stop.

"You are only five seconds behind Alec Bennett, who is leading," his mechanic Peter Betts shouted in his ear.

"Freddie is at least ten seconds behind you." Frank accepted the clean pair of goggles Pete handed him. He was relieved to be able to see clearly again. The old goggles were covered with dead flies and streaks of engine grease. With dust and oil build-up, his face became a dirty black mask.

"No problem, I'm going to win this race," Frank shouted back to Pete as he slammed the petrol cap shut and roared off again. Frank was confident there were a couple of corners he could take even quicker to make up that time. Frank tucked his body down low over the petrol tank and wound the throttle flat out. Down the hill to Kirk Michael Corner, he went through faster than ever before, smiling to himself as he brushed the left-hand verge. This was 15 miles round the final lap.

I'm nearly halfway, he thought, I can really do this. Powerfully out of Ramsey Hairpin, his self-built engine was running beautifully. It was just touching the flint wall inside the bend as he leant the bike in, climbing up Snaefell, the 30-mile marker.

Frank was in the zone, completely at one with his cherished Norton, with the engine screaming flat out through the sweeping curves of Bungalow and Windy Corners. For a second, he allowed himself to dream of victory…he could even picture the Hermes, winged silver trophy.

With only two miles to go, on the descent to Cregny-Baa, Frank turned his Norton into the right-hand bend fractionally too fast. He intuitively knew that he was in trouble. The Norton ran a few inches wide, offline by just three inches, the difference between glory and disaster.

Frank's beloved motorbike slid onto the loose gravel at the edge of the road, now he was riding on. Fighting desperately for control, for a split second he felt relief as he thought he had saved it, but in that instant the rear wheel slipped off the edge of the road. His wonderful dream was becoming his worst nightmare.

With the violent movement of the bike Frank fell left from its leather seat and with arms and legs flailing he fell down the 40-foot drop in a graceful arc. Halfway down the mountainside his body hit, right knee first, against a large, grey granite boulder, the impact ripping his racing leathers open as they caught on the jagged rock.

Fortunately, this slowed his progress a little, but his right kneecap had been shattered against the unyielding ancient hard rock.

Years later, Frank would clearly remember that moment every time he tapped and broke the shell of his boiled egg at breakfast. A deep gulley eventually arrested his free fall partway down the steep slope. On impact his right leg folded under him and snapped like a braking twig. Instantly looking up he saw his Norton fly over him, just a foot above his head. With a sickening crunching scream, it slammed into another large, granite outcrop. With a final loud hiss, like a dying man's last breath, the poor Norton's remains came to a sickening, smoking, steaming halt.

Then the pain kicked in and Frank Cartland passed out.

Chapter Thirteen

The Moncrieff's wealth had been accumulated in the cotton mills of Lancashire. Simon Moncrieff was the third-generation owner of Moncrieff's Mills in Preston. At fifty years old, Simon had been a widower for five years when Alice Morris seduced him with charm and beauty.

Alice, only twenty-one when they first met, knew her beauty's effect on men, and she fully intended to use all her charms. The Morris family worked as shopkeepers, with Alice's father and his brother running two shops close to Moncrieff's Mills. Much of the shop custom generated from the mill workers.

Alice knew exactly what she wanted out of life. She had no intention of spending it stuck in Preston with a family of screaming children like her sister and cousins. She needed a rich husband, and widower Simon Moncrieff was her target. Alice ensured that Simon noticed her from his carriage as it passed her father's shop on his many visits to his mills.

Despite his family's protests, Simon quickly became besotted with Alice Morris, and she soon snared her man. The couple were married at St Stephen Church in Warrington on 20th August 1900.

Simon had two sons from his first marriage. Both were now in their twenties, just a few years older than his new wife. They saw Alice precisely for what she was - a gold digger - and they hated her. To placate the boys, Simon handed over the control of the family mills to them, leaving him free to attempt to keep his new, young wife contented.

With Alice's pressure, Simon purchased a large old manor house in Cheshire, and their lavish parties soon became famed throughout the county.

Simon and Alice were delighted when their daughter Silvia was born in 1902. Alice had just one ambition for her daughter from birth: marrying her into a titled old English family.

With no cotton mills to occupy his time, gambling became Simon Moncrieff's real passion in life. Alice soon realised this would be an excellent opportunity to pursue her ambitions for Silvia. With Alice's encouragement, Simon joined some of the best London gentleman's clubs.

In the Mayfair Club, while playing roulette, he was first introduced to Lord John Marshall, a fellow hardened gambler. It had not been a chance meeting. Alice had arranged for the Honourable Richard Mears, one of her London lovers, to bring the two men together.

The war had somewhat stalled her ambitions, but to Alice's delight, the Moncrieff family received an invite to the Marshall Box at the 1919 Epsom Derby. It was the first Derby since the war, and an enormous crowd had gathered on Epsom Downs.

Both John Marshall and Simon Moncrieff had large bets on the race, with Lord Marshall placing £100 on the horse of his friend Lord Derby. Simon Moncrieff placed £100 on a horse called Grand Parade, trained in Ireland. He had seen the horse winning a good race the previous year. Grand Parade was the outsider.

"Your horse has no chance; he has been injured; didn't you know?" said John Marshall smugly to Simon as the horses lined up behind the starting tapes. Only the bookmakers and Simon were pleased when Grand Parade won The Derby by three lengths at 33:1, winning Simon Moncrieff £3,300.

"He doesn't need the bloody money," said a disgusted John Marshall to his wife as he tore up his losing ticket.

"Thank you for the invitation, John. It has been a delightful day. I will buy you all dinner and champagne tonight," Simon said to John Marshall as they left the track.

"Should think you bloody will", muttered Lord Marshall in response.

It was at Epsom that George and Silvia met for the first time. Now seventeen, Silvia had become a beautiful and spirited young lady. At 5 feet 7 inches tall, slim, with long, silk-like, raven-black hair and dark brown eyes, it was fair to say that her looks were stunning. She had inherited her mother's seduction skills, and George was immediately under her spell. "H…hello, Silvia", George said when his mother introduced him to her, and he shook her soft, smooth hand.

Ever since the experiences with his brothers, George was afraid to look any of the servant girls in the eye. The feelings stirring inside him from the shock of touching this beautiful new girl felt terrific.

Alice had already turned her daughter into an experienced young woman, having encouraged one of her own lovers to seduce Silvia and take her virginity when she was just sixteen. The following day, Silvia had said,

"Thank you, Mother," and smiling, added, "I'm glad that's out of the way. You can have him back now." Alice had primed Silvia before the meeting at Epsom, ensuring she encouraged any interest from George. This is something that Silvia was happy to do

The Moncrieff's wealth had been accumulated in the cotton mills of Lancashire. Simon Moncrieff was the third-generation owner of "What do you think of him?" said Alice to her daughter when they were alone watching the racehorse's parade in the paddock. Admiring the gleaming athletic animals moving effortlessly passed her Silva said with a confident smile.
"Rather disappointing to look at, but I'm sure I can turn him into something presentable,"
The mothers of both families were happy. George's apparent interest in Silvia delighted Victoria Marshall, and this development was precisely as she had planned it.
Victoria saw marriage into the Moncrieff family, with the vast fortune she knew that Silvia would eventually inherit, as the best chance to ensure financial security for the Marshall dynasty. Judging by seventy year-old Simon Moncrieff's aged appearance, she reckoned that the inheritance would come very soon, this prospect made her smile.
The year was 1920, and the Brooklands motor course was reopening. George and Silvia, accompanied by their parents, attended the first race meeting. This was George's second visit to the course.
"I'll show you around if you like," he told Silvia.
"Thank you, George, that would be lovely," Silvia replied.
George was thrilled to find Silvia's attention focused on him, but the attention she drew from others, both men and women, unsettled him. He was unaccustomed to being the centre of attention.
"I'm going to race cars here as soon as I get my money," he excitedly told her. "My grandfather left me

£5000, which will be available when I reach twenty-one."

Silva gave him lovely smile.

"If we marry George, we could get a racing car together much sooner than that, "she said

Her comment left George in a state of shock.

"I ... I would really like that Silvia, but I will have to ask mother first," his blurted reply.

Inwardly, Silvia couldn't help but feel a mix of amusement and disdain at George's naivety. His obvious weakness, however, also pleased her. The thought of the power she could soon hold excited her. Once married to her, George would be nothing more than a puppet in her hands.

The Moncrieff's, especially Alice, were extremely happy for the relationship to develop, as marrying into the old Marshall family would fulfil her dreams. When George returned to Sefton Manor after the trip to Brooklands, he found his mother alone in the drawing room.

"Mother," he said nervously, "I have decided that I would like to get married."

Victoria had, of course, expected this conversation. She and Alice Moncrieff agreed it would be a satisfactory arrangement for both families. "Who is the young lady? I hope she is from a good family?" said Victoria, feigning surprise.

"It… it's Silvia Moncrieff, the girl at Brooklands," stammered George.

"She is certainly very pretty; I must discuss it with your father when he returns from London."

Victoria was delighted. Silvia Moncrieff's money would be the answer to the Marshall financial worries. Victoria put George out of his misery two days later. He had been moping around the manor and looking at her expectantly every time she walked into the room.

"Very well, George, you have our blessing. You may ask Silvia Moncrieff to marry you,".

"Oh, thank you, Mother," said a delighted George. He went across the room and tried to give his mother a hug. Victoria immediately stepped away…as if her son had some infectious disease.

George proposed to Silvia on Christmas Eve 1920 as the two families met for drinks at The Ritz. Later in the evening, an anxious and slightly drunk George managed to get Silvia alone.

"I…I would like to marry you, Silva… If you will have me".

"This is my answer, George," she said, wrapping her arms around him and kissing him passionately on the lips.

The couple married in April 1921, and all members of both families were happy—for a short while at least.

The marriage, a lavish affair, was. Held at Sefton Manor. Alice Moncrieff, still a gorgeous woman, wanted to demonstrate her new position in society, so she invited more than one hundred of her northern family and friends to the wedding, much to the dismay of Victoria Marshall. "They are all so uncouth," she said to Lady Roseberry, one of her guests. "I cannot understand a word most of them are saying." They may as well be talking in a foreign language."

The contrast with the 'old' families invited by the Marshalls was striking.

Simon Moncrieff was now rather a pathetic figure. At seventy-two, his health had suffered markedly over the previous two years. His discomfort was evident to everyone watching him slowly walk his daughter down the aisle. Gout and arthritis were giving him great pain. During the wedding, the official photographer asked,

"Please come here, sir, and stand beside your beautiful granddaughter."

Alice had found this extremely amusing.

George was delighted with the newlyweds' first night together. It was undoubtedly one of the most pleasant experiences of his life.

His father had surprised him at the wedding reception by handing him a book. It had a worn, red leather cover with the words Kama Sutra embossed in faded and flaking gold letters.

"This little book was given to me by my uncle when I was your age," Lord Marshall explained. "It has served me very well", he said, winking at his son. "Make sure you study it, boy".

After a short, awkward silence, he shook George's hand, turned, and returned to his drinking cronies.

Those were the most words his father had ever said to George.

Since his early traumatic experience with his brothers, sex was something that made George extremely nervous, and boarding school had confused him even more. Several boys experimented on each other. George was always too afraid to join in.

Silvia, on the other hand, knew exactly what to do and soon took him in her hands. Delighted to see the book, she enthusiastically read the Kama Sutra.

"How wonderful of your father to give us this book. I think it's the best wedding present we've had," she said. "I'll have to thank him myself."

George was worried that she didn't appear to be joking.

Silvia soon led George in experimenting with many of the more unusual positions described in the book, but unfortunately, his lack of fitness and stamina often left her frustrated.

The Marshall and Moncrieff families were delighted when Silvia fell pregnant only six months after the wedding.

George and Silvia had set up a home at the Lodge House on the manor's grounds. With three stories, five bedrooms and a castellated roof, it was certainly large enough for them.

This will do until I get my hands on that old manor, thought Silvia.

Their first child was born on June 3, 1922, a healthy boy whom they named William John Marshall. Silvia was relieved when she noticed that baby William looked much more like her than George, although he did have the Marshall blond hair.

With substantial pressure from his wife and considerable envy from Victoria Marshall, Simon Moncrieff had been buying all the latest, top-class motor cars.

Silvia, having been well taught by her mother in the art of persuasion, used her charm on her father and said,

"All our friends have Bentleys now, Daddy. Is it about the time George and I had one? It would be the best present ever."

After a week of constant requests from his daughter, he gave in.

"Very well, my girl," he said. "I'll leave you to choose the best model for your growing family." Just three days later, Silvia drove back to Sefton Lodge, shattering the peace of the country estate with the bellowing exhaust note of a 1923 dark green racing Bentley.

Knowing Silvia was out, Victoria Marshall had taken the opportunity to call at the lodge. For more than an hour, she nagged her son.

"It's time you took control of that women you married George. You really must take charge." You let her do whatever she wants. Her place is at home looking after you and our grandson William."

George was silent under his mother's harassing but wished he had the strength to tell her what he was thinking. *You didn't look after me when I was growing up.* Were his thoughts.

He was thankful to hear a loud engine noise outside. Silvia had arrived home.

As George and his mother hurried outside to see what was causing all the noise; a spray of gravel scattered around their feet.

Ignoring her mother-in-law, Silvia said.
"Jump in, Georgie," she said as she slid the large machine to a stop. We are going to take this old thing to Brooklands."

Without hesitation George jumped into the passenger seat, and, in a further shower of gravel, Silvia roared away.

The privileged young couples were off to turn their Brooklands dreams into reality. They left an open-mouthed and angry Victoria Marshall who could only watch in despair.

Chapter Fourteen

George was happy to win a few small handicap races at Brooklands. But his satisfaction was tempered. Much to his discomfort, Silvia, although not allowed to race, proved she could lap the great concrete bowl faster him when she tested their Bentley.

"It is stupid these stuffy old committee men will not allow us girls to race around here. There are at least six of us who can beat most of you men. I am going to form a pressure group to force them to change the rules."

"They will not listen to you." George had told her, but he knew that remark was true.

"They bloody well will." Had been her response.

With the money Simon Moncrieff had been paying him for road cars and the fact that George was, at least, a competent driver, W. O. Bentley invited George to join the Bentley team at the 1925 Le Mans 24-hour race as a reserve driver. For that honour, Mr. Bentley would charge George £500 to cover all their expenses.

"Sounds like an awful lot of money, and I'm not sure I have enough experience." A doubtful George said to Silvia.

"Rubbish you will be fine. It will show just how good a racing driver you are." She had answered. *But I expect you will make a fool of yourself.* She thought.

Silvia went with George, leaving two-year-old William at the lodge with his nanny.

Les Vingt-Quatre Heures Du Mans was first run in May 1923, when a green Bentley finished 5th. They had entered just one car in 1924 and won the race. A confident W.O. Bentley entered four cars for the 1925 race, hoping to ensure another victory.

Much to the relief of George the ferry crossing from Dover to Calais was smooth. Both were in good spirits as they started the drive down through northern France in their touring Bentley.

All the Bentley team drivers had planned an overnight stop at the Hotel Le Maurice in Paris to begin their Le Mans adventure. After a champagne-fuelled dinner, the whole party went next door to the Revue Bar, which was considered the most outrageous club in Paris. The star performer was an exotic dancer, Hellen Dupery, whose lithe, barely clothed body, cropped blond hair, and wide smile captivated all who saw her.
Especially George Marshall.

"My, Georgie, I've not seen you this excited since our wedding night," Silvia whispered to him with amusement.

"I ... I just think she is a lovely dancer," said a red-faced George. Silvia was delighted to see him so animated. *Maybe this will give him more stamina in bed tonight*, she thought. Hellen was invited back to the Bentley table after her performance, and much to the surprise and delight of all, she told them she would also be at Le Mans for the race.

"I plan to race there myself very soon," Hellen announced.

"So do I," said Silvia excitedly. "We should race there together." Everyone thought this was a splendid idea …everyone except George.

Returning from the Revue Bar around 2am, they went straight to bed. While they lay in the single beds in their Paris hotel room, an intoxicated George slurred,

"Women are not allowed to drive in the Le Mans 24-hour race. You need stamina and strength to handle a racing car for that length of time."

Silvia said nothing; she clenched her jaw as she always did when angry. *I'll show you, Georgie Porgy, if that's what's needed, you are not going to last five minutes.* she thought.

An extreme excess of champagne made sure George wasn't fit to put up any sort of performance that night.

Silvia lay in bed, frustrated and unable to sleep. She already loved this new, exciting race and hadn't even seen the race circuit yet. She also found the dashing, daring, worldly Bentley team drivers extremely attractive.

Now, finding a like-minded, strong-willed woman like Hellen seemed so perfect. Silvia was growing tired of George, who never seemed confident and was always afraid to upset his mother.

The "Bentley Boys" were all wealthy, experienced racing drivers. They were all men full of confidence, and she knew they were all mesmerized by her style and beauty. Seducing one of these boys will be child's play, she thought, becoming aroused at the very idea.

She looked at George and sighed. He already had his mouth open and was snoring lightly. She would pleasure herself to sleep again tonight.

Dawn on practice day arrived, a gap in the curtains allowed a light-yellow glow to spread across Marshall's bedroom. Knowing he would be driving fast laps on this challenging and dangerous Le Mans track, George had woken bathed in sweat around 3 am and could not get back to sleep.

At 7 am, Silvia heard the load retching sound of George being sick in the bathroom next to their room. "What's the matter, Georgie? If you are this nervous, you shouldn't be driving today. Shall we ask Mr. Bentley if I can drive instead of you?" she shouted.

Coming out of the bathroom, wrapped in a white hotel towel that contrasted sharply with his pink body and red face, George angrily replied,

"Of course not. I am fine; I must have eaten something bad last night, that's all. Think it was the lobster."

Silvia always called him Georgie when she was annoyed with him. She knew he hated it and that it reminded him of his long-dead brothers. She thought *fat red lobster would be a good name for you.*

Once all the regular drivers had finished their qualifying laps, George was allowed out for his run in the Bentley.

A lap of the Le Mans track was 10.726 miles. It was narrow and largely tree lined. Its surface, dusty in fine weather and very slippery when wet.

The 3.0 litre Bentley was the most powerful and fastest car George had ever driven. After instruction and advice from team driver Alexander Dumar, he eased into the brown leather driving seat, strapped on his white leather helmet, and pulled down his goggles.

George gripped the large steering wheel tightly to ensure Silvia and Hellen, standing next to the car, wouldn't notice his hands shaking. With a swift pull down to the right on the large wooden wheel, he turned the green car out of the pits and was off on his Le Mans adventure.

The engine note changed from a purr to a growl as George accelerated the Bentley down the straight, narrow road into the outskirts of Le Mans town and approached the first corner, the slow Pontlieue Hairpin bend. Braking hard and slowing down to just 30mph, he turned sharp right before entering the Mulsanne Straight, which George said after his drive, "Went on and on forever".

With increasing speed on the long, long straight, the Bentley, even with George driving, reached 120mph. Rounding the slight right-hand kink towards the end of the straight, George noticed the marker boards for the fast-approaching Mulsanne Corner. He lifted his right foot off the throttle and stamped it hard onto the brakes for the tight corner, careful not to touch the sand bank on the outside. He got safely around at just 40mph.

Accelerating out of the corner into a funnel of trees, which seemed to suck him along, he raced flat out for another mile down to the right and left turns at Indianapolis Corner. Following a quick blast of acceleration, he again pressed hard on the brake pedal to slow down for the ninety-degree right-hand corner at Arnage. Then, immediately his right foot pressed down for full throttle, and he was heading to the fast and scary curves at the White House.

As he rushed along the narrow grey road toward the bends, with the mass of trees a green blur to each side of him, George recalled Alexander Dumar boasting that it takes real guts to go through these blind bends without lifting your right foot off the throttle.

Even on that first lap, George knew he would never be able to do that.

From the White House, he drove flat out once more for over a mile until he flashed past the pits to start another high-speed lap.

George enjoyed the five laps experience, although his best lap was over two minutes slower than the Bentley team drivers.

That night, alone in his bed, George became depressed thinking about his laps of the Le Mans circuit. For the first time in his life, he was aware that he would never be a top-class racing driver. He had scared himself on every lap through the fast curves, especially at the White House, and after his five laps, he was completely exhausted.

Silvia had said nothing to him after his run, but Hellen, who had been watching from the pits, said, "Well done, George, you look dashing behind the wheel." Then she planted a soft, wet kiss full on his lips. Now, licking his lips, George thought that was the day's best moment.

He thought of Hellen as he drifted off to sleep.

It was sweltering, almost tropical, for the Le Mans 24 hours that year, but Bentley won the race after much drama and challenging racing. Of course, there were wild celebrations that evening. Silvia, having drunk too much, ended up in the bed of Alexander Dumar, one of the winning drivers.

Watching his wife go off with Alexander, an angry and champagne-fuelled George took one of the , young French girls who had been invited to the party back to his hotel room for the night. But it was not a success. Despite her helping hands, George was unable to perform. His mind and lusts were elsewhere.

Hellen didn't stay for the party; she had to rush back to Paris to perform her dancing duties.

"I will come to England soon, George," she said before she left. "Be sure to look me up." She then kissed him before jumping into her borrowed Talbot Darracq car.

From the moment of that tender kiss, Hellen consumed George's every thought. His desire for her was intense, a flame that burned brighter with each passing day.

The Le Mans weekend marked the beginning of George and Silvia's open marriage, a practice readily accepted in the society they frequented. It was a time when affairs were not uncommon, a response to the post-war era's harshness and deprivation. The need for fun, music, and excitement was palpable, especially in the wealthy set of the early twenties.
Silvia was in great demand by all the privileged, wealthy, and smart young men of London society.

In 1925, Silvia found herself pregnant again. In February 1926, just nine months after their eventful Le Mans trip, she gave birth to a healthy, dark-haired baby girl they named Victoria. The fact that Victoria bore no resemblance to George was a topic never broached in the Marshall family. Still, it didn't stop the tabloids from speculating on her true paternity.

The young Marshall's were a newsworthy couple, but Silvia didn't care what the reporters wrote, and George pretended not to notice.

Chapter Fifteen

It was fortunate for Frank that Howard Jones had travelled to the Isle of Man in 1927. Howard wanted to be there to witness the proud moment of Frank's glory.

Doctor Jones was able to organise a private room and the best possible treatment for his injured young friend. The hospital has been busy this year. Two riders had been killed, and seven were in hospital, including Frank, with broken bones.

After the race, with Frank safely in hospital, Howard Jones went with Peter to collect the crashed Norton from the accident site.

After information from locals who witnessed the accident Peter stopped the van at the edge of the road where Frank's dreams had been destroyed.

It was around 8 p.m. before they found the bike. Forty feet down the steep slope below the bleak mountain road. A gusty wind was driving fine salty rain from the sea, and it was getting dark. With an involuntary cry Peter slumped down on a granite bolder when he saw the wreak of the Norton laying like discarded scrap metal among the rough heather.

"The bastards, they have stolen the engine. That was the best engine Frank had ever built," he said before tears overwhelmed him.

Doctor Jones put his arm around Peter's shoulder. "Don't worry, Pete, you know Frank will be back. He's a real fighter."
Then the sad pair struggled to haul the black remains back up the slippery steep slope.
This would be impossible if they hadn't stolen the engine. Howard thought

Privately, having seen the damage to Frank's knee, Howard was aware that the patella bone had been fractured in three places. Frank would be lucky to walk again. He would indeed never have enough strength in his leg to race a motorbike.

Howard had sent a telegram to Joan telling her about the accident and that Frank's injuries were severe but not life-threatening. The following morning, after ensuring Frank was comfortable, the two despondent men travelled home in the van with the sad remains of the Norton dumped in the back. It was a sombre, slow journey.

Howard Jones had never married. Growing up in Lancashire, he had won a scholarship to Cambridge University to study medicine. When Howard qualified, he wanted to stay in East Anglia. He had no plans to return to his northern industrial roots. After his graduation, he spent some time looking around for work.

In September 1905, old Doctor McKenzie, who had run the practice covering the villages of Farewell, Burlham and two other small villages a few miles outside Cambridge for over thirty years, died after suffering a heart attack.

The Cambridge Evening News advertised a post for a new doctor, and the newly qualified Doctor Jones applied, more in hope than any expectation. Much to his surprise, he was accepted for the job after a short interview.

The doctor's house he was allocated to, The Cedars, was in Farewell. The Cedars was a large, four bedroom brick property built in the early nineteenth century. One of its downstairs rooms had been converted into a surgery and another into a waiting room. Doctor Jones had a housekeeper and a cook inherited from

Doctor McKenzie. Both middle-aged women were set in their ways, and they ran the house between them.

Howard came from a family where his mother had dominated his every move, so the arrangement felt quite natural to him.

With his slight fear of women, Howard was not looking forward to meeting Joan and Margaret when he returned from the Isle of Man.

The first time he had contact with the Cartland family was soon after he arrived when Joan visited the surgery in 1906. She held the hand of a skinny little boy who had his left arm in a sling. When Howard saw Joan, his heart had given a little jump. She looked like a young version of his mother.

"Hello, young man, you look a bit worse for wear, Howard had said to the boy, who looked down at the floor and said nothing.

"His name is Frank," explained Joan. "My youngest brother, he has fallen over and hurt his arm."

"Let's look at you then, Frank," said Doctor Jones. "Please take your shirt off."

Joan helped Frank out of the sling and his shirt.

"My...you seem to have been in the wars, Frank," Howard Jones said. He tried not to show his surprise at the number of bruises covering Frank's body.

"Let's have a look at this arm."

Frank hadn't uttered a word as the doctor examined it.

"You haven't broken your arm, lad, so that's good news. I'll give you a new sling. Keep it there for a week, then come back to see me. Now, wait outside while I have a chat with your sister."

Frank went and sat on a chair in the waiting room. On the table, he saw a magazine with the word Autocar in large letters written on the cover, which also had a picture of a strange, horseless carriage racing along a dusty road.

Inside the surgery, Doctor Jones said,

"I'm rather concerned about all those bruises on your brother's body, Miss ... sorry, could you tell me your name?"

"I'm Joan Cartland, Doctor. Frank is always getting into scrapes. You know what young boys are like. " Hesitantly Howard asked.

"Are you sure that's where he has got all the marks?"

"Yes, I'm sure," said Joan sharply. She was too afraid of her father to tell Howard Jones the truth.

Not wishing to alarm her, Howard Jones said, as he opened the surgery door for Joan,

"Well, please bring him back next week. I would like to see how his arm is healing." They were surprised to see Frank still engrossed in the Autocar magazine.

"You can take that with you if you like, Frank," said Howard Jones.

"Really!" said Frank excitedly. "Tha...thank you, Doctor Jones." Joan had given Howard Jones a big smile as she followed her little brother out of The Cedars.

    From that first meeting, Howard Jones had been in love with Joan, but he had always been too shy to ask her out. Now, more than ten years had passed since she had lost her only love, Norman Crowe. Those years had not been kind to her, but to Howard, she was still the handsome young woman he had first fallen in love with. Following Frank's accident, though, for once, he wasn't looking forward to seeing Joan.

His first call was to Ivy Cottage to see Margaret; with relief, he found that Joan was there with her. This meant he wouldn't have to face the two angry women separately and could answer all their questions at once.

"Tell us the truth. Is Frank going to live?" Margaret said, opening the door before Howard had time to knock.

He told the concerned women.

"Yes, he is, but it will be a slow recovery. They will keep him in the Isle of Man hospital for at least two more weeks."

The pain, misery and self-pity, that Frank felt for the two days after the accident were intense. The recognition that one small mistake had cost him dearly was hard to bear. He'd been so close to victory and that one thought continued to dominate his mind.

The only release he could get from the severe pain in his knee came from the regular doses of morphine he was given. The sensation of euphoria as the needle injected the magic liquid into his veins was undoubtedly addictive. He could feel the shooting pain easing and drifting away, giving his mind freedom.

I'm rushing down the track, throttle twisted wide open. My eyes are unblinking and focused on the narrow strip of road ahead. Trees, walls, and a blur of people flash by. The Norton engine is singing to me once again.
We are going to win
We are going to win

We are going to win
I roar across the finishing line as the chequered flag comes down.
The crowd cheers, and the champagne flows as I lift the TT winner's Silver Trophy...

A sharp pain shoots through Frank's knee, returning him to reality. "Nurse, nurse, please come here quick. I need more morphine, now." This became his regular desperate appeal.

Frank had to spend three weeks in the Isle of Man hospital. His shattered kneecap required two extended operations to wire the bones back together. He also had to have his leg pinned and set before he was transported back to Addenbrooks Hospital in Cambridge. With a lift from Doctor Jones in his new Morris Minor saloon car, Joan brought Mary and little sister Emily to visit their father in the Cambridge hospital.

"Is your motorbike hurt as well". The first thing Mary said to her father.

With watery eyes, Franks replied

"It is my dear girl...even more than me, I'm afraid".

Margaret had refused to visit the hospital while Frank made his long, slow recovery.

On his return home a few weeks later, Frank was enthusiastically welcomed by Mary and especially by Spike. Even though he was now seventeen years old, Spike excitedly performed his party trick—jumping high in the air and howling.

Margaret's reception was, however, much as he expected.

"You bloody fool," she said when the girls were out of earshot. "I hope this has taught you a lesson."

Dejectedly, Frank shuffled off into his quiet, dark workshop. Standing just inside the door, leaning on his wooden walking stick, Frank looked over to the corner of the room. The remains of his beautiful Norton were leaning against a bench.

It was the first time he had seen the bike since the moment he had passed out on Isle of Man Mountain. His last thoughts had been of relief that the bike had stopped and didn't look too bad. Now he saw that the impact with the granite boulder had turned the Norton's chassis banana shaped. Pete had already informed him that the engine had been stolen.

It's only suitable for scrap metal now, he thought. *Even I can't repair that.*

With his right knee hurting like hell, it was at that moment when Frank knew he would never race a motorbike again. The Isle of Man TT win would remain a dream as it had always been. Depressed, he turned and returned to the cottage to give Margaret the news.

"Margaret. I'm sure you will be pleased to know that I've ridden in my last motorcycle race," he said with evident sadness. Seeing his obvious distress, she replied with rare compassion. "Oh, Frank, you know I'm pleased. I've been waiting five years for you to say that. Maybe I can stop worrying about you every day, and we can enjoy a normal family life."

Frank's announcement delighted Margaret. Now that his wild days were over forever, she would have him home for good.

While stuck in hospital, Frank was lucky his young mechanic, Pete Betts, could run the garage for him. Pete shared Frank's love for mechanical things. Pete was the youngest son of farmer Albert Betts but preferred the garage to the farm. Pete kept the garage open and sold petrol while Frank was recovering. This at least brought some money in for the Cartland family.

However, Frank was comforted knowing that Margaret's father would never see his family starve. They would always have bread to eat but he knew he would have to return to hard work and start building plenty of new engines.

Frank concentrated on building up the garage business for the following months and keeping his customers happy. As his injuries slowly healed, all thoughts of racing were banished to the back of his mind. Watching Margaret washing up after dinner one evening, Frank thought she must have been having too much of her father's lovely fresh bread. He was sure she was plumper than when he returned home a few weeks earlier. In bed that night, Margaret had some news for him.

"I am expecting another baby," she said. It's due in about six months. I've already told my parents, and they are delighted."

"So am I ..." said Frank without much conviction. He loved his two girls but realised that another new baby would cause Margaret even more stress and sleepless nights.

While Margaret peacefully slumbered, Frank, tormented by his thoughts, sought solace in the tranquil confines of his workshop. This haven was his sanctuary, a place where he could escape the confusion of his mind and immerse himself in what truly mattered-his engines.

Seated at the workbench, Frank contemplated that this was the one place where he still held control of his life. Here, he could lose himself for hours, meticulously polishing and balancing the jewel-like pistons and connecting rods, honing the cylinder bores until they were silky-smooth, and lovingly rebuilding his precious engines. These were not just machines to him. They were his babies, each one a testament to his skill and dedication, and he cared for them as a parent would for their child.

Chapter Sixteen

The permanent legacy of the Isle of Man accident was that Frank would always walk as if he had a large stone stuck inside his right shoe.

On a Wednesday lunchtime Frank hobbled down to the Railway Arms, with Joe taking his arm on one side and Spike limping along on the other side. This trio made a sad sight as they painfully hobbled and limped down to the pub.

Joan had been to the cemetery to put flowers on their mother's grave. Had she lived, she would have been sixty years old on that very day. Walking back to the forge, Joan noticed her boys from the top of the lane. She stood and watched them with sadness as they slowly descended towards the Railway Arms.

What has life done to us all? Joan thought. *Those three would have been laughing, joking, and running to the pub ten years ago. Now, those carefree days are long gone.*

Sighing, she turned and returned to the empty and dark forge cottage.

Almost everyone in Burlham loved Spike. From his puppy days as the bookie's runner's assistant, travelling with Frank in the wire basket of their old green bike, he had made friends with all who met him. His bark really was worse than his bite, although the bullyboys of Farewell would always have a different opinion. They still bore the scars of Spike's anger.

Even the village butcher, Alan Coles, who was forever chasing Spike away from his back door, had a soft spot for him. Butcher Coles had been one of Frank's best customers when he was a bookie's runner; Spike always had his eye on the strings of pork sausages hanging behind the shop counter. One day, while Frank and Alan were discussing the bets Alan wanted to place, Spike sneaked out of his basket and stole some sausages. The string was six sausages long, almost too big for Spike's tiny mouth, but he managed and set off for home.

"Come back, you cheeky little mutt," the butcher shouted as he set off in hot pursuit. Spike ran as fast as his short legs allowed. They tangled with the bouncing sausages, but despite that handicap, Spike was fortunately too fast for the well-fed butcher, and he scampered back to Forge cottage.

Once there he hid under Frank's old bed and enjoyed his meal. Spike was in the doghouse for a few days, but the sausages had been worth it.

In the snug bar at The Railway Arms, Spike had his own seat. It was a tired-looking, old, white wicker chair; no one else dared to sit in it if they thought there was any chance Spike might be coming into the pub. That Wednesday, After Joe and Frank had had their two pints of mild, and Spike had enjoyed two ashtrays full of his favourite rich, dark stout, the men sat smoking their Woodbines, with the dog curled up in his chair next to them.

All in a happy silence. Their peace was only disturbed when the landlord, Dan Turner, rang the bell and said,

"Time, gentlemen, please".

"Right, you two, it's two o'clock. Time we were making our way home," Frank said. "I've got an engine to build this afternoon."

Joe and Frank got up, but Spike didn't move.

"Come on, Spike, you lazy old dog," said Joe, giving him a poke. Spike still didn't move.

"Drunk too much beer, have you, sozzled old dog? I suppose I'm going to have to carry you home," said Frank, putting his arm under Spike to pick him up.

Realisation that his old companion had died in his sleep hit Frank like a hammer blow.
The brothers, both in tears, slowly carried their little friend back home to the forge.

For many years, Spike's bed had been an old motorcycle tyre covered in a dirty grey blanket next to the range in the kitchen. They gently laid him in it and left him for the rest of the day. Curled up, he looked as if he were just fast asleep. Joan gave an agitated and distressed Joe some of the pills Doctor Jones had prescribed to help him calm down, and she sat with him as he cried himself to sleep.

When Margaret noticed Frank approaching Ivy Cottage shuffling along, head down and with a red tearful face. She went out to meet him.

"What the hell has happen now" she said sharply.

"My Spike died today in the pub. I know he has lived to a great age for a dog, but I'm really going to miss him … he was my best friend."

You always loved that bloody little dog more than me, Margaret thought.

Joe decided that Spike should be buried on the Devil's Dyke, overlooking the racecourse.

"That's the place he always loved best," he said, tears trickling down his cheeks once again. "He loved spending the day chasing rabbits and just sitting on the high bank for hours with me."

Everyone agreed that this would be the best place for the burial, and on a sharp but clear autumn day in 1927, they walked with Spike's body for the three miles to the site Joe had chosen.

The turn out amazed Frank. Besides the Cartland family, another ten people made the long walk, including Doctor Jones, Constable Clarke and even the butcher Alan Cope, who joked that at least his pork sausages would be safe.

More people have come here for Spike than came for the funerals of Charlie or John. He reflected.

Chapter Seventeen

The following two years saw gradual recovery for Frank, both physically and financially.

His engine-building skills were still in great demand from his motorcycle-racing customers, and the more races they won, the number of riders desiring to use a Cartland-built engines increased. With engines and motorbikes scattered everywhere, Frank was fast outgrowing his village garage and workshop.

Without the significant expense of his own racing, the family was gradually becoming better off. Margaret had given birth to their third child, a girl whom they named Edith after her aunt. In addition to caring for the family's needs, Margaret chased all the customers who still needed to pay their bills. This job suited her blunt, black-and-white approach to life. For the moment, the Cartland household was a happy one.

"You really are outnumbered in this family, Frank," said a laughing Howard Jones one day. "Now you've got four women to nag you... no, five, counting your sister Joan."

"At least there should be someone here to look after me when I'm old and past it, "replied Frank with a grin.

After his accident on the Isle of Man and then Spike's death, Frank's once optimistic enthusiasm for life had diminished. He had lost much of his old spark, but now Howard had noticed that some of his friend's positivity had returned.

He knew Frank had begun reading motor magazines again and excitedly talking about racing cars and bikes to anyone who would listen.

Although the limp was still pronounced, he could also see positive improvements in Frank's health.

"I can't imagine you will ever grow old," Howard told him.

Inwardly, he realised that the accident had done little to quell his friend's speed addiction. It simmered just waiting for a new outlet.

This opportunity would come at the expense of Margaret's steady, happy family life. Early on an April morning in 1930, the sleepy village peace of Burlham was shattered by the arrival Freddie O'Hare. Freddie turned up at Frank's garage with a noisy and speedy new silver Frazer Nash Ulster sports car.

He had a proposition for Frank.

"You know how every bugger wants to use your engines, fearless? Well, a work shed next to mine is now empty at Brooklands. It's a great bloody chance to build your engines at the track; how about joining me? Also, I need a new riding mechanic; you would be great for the job. I'll give you ten per cent of the prize money."

Two seasons previously, Freddie had retired from motorcycle racing and had started car racing. Immediately, he became remarkably successful with his special chain-drive Frazer Nash cars, beating many of the more powerful racing cars and their established wealthy Brooklands drivers.

Although his skills as a driver and engineer meant that Freddie was accepted by the upper-class society of the Brooklands establishment, it was a reluctant acceptance. His irreverent approach to life and poor background always made his presence uncomfortable for the privileged majority.

Freddie neglected to tell Frank that he had the workshop space and needed a new riding mechanic because his last one had just been killed while racing a motorbike in Ireland.

"You don't bloody well expect me to be a passenger again after what happened at Spa, do you?" said Frank

"Don't be daft, it's different in a car; completely safe. All you need to do is look out for faster cars coming past us on the banking, those bloody great Bentleys and Lagondas. There wouldn't be many; you know I'm the best bloody driver out there."

Feeling the flutter of excitement building in his stomach, without another thought, Frank replied,

"Okay, Freddie. Let's go and take a look at this workshop."

As he eased himself into the Frazer Nash, Frank shouted across to Pete Betts, who had come out to admire the Nash.

"Look after the place, Pete...oh, and tell Margaret I'll be back this evening." Freddie engaged first gear, floored the throttle, and the 1.5-litre engine snarled, rushing them down the long, twisting, and dusty roads south to Brooklands. Once again, Frank excitedly left home to follow his love for motors and speed.

Margaret watched from the kitchen window with growing anger as her husband sped away and again felt helpless.

Selfish, bloody thoughtless, fool, she thought.

But inside, she had always known that Frank would put his passion for racing and engines before his family whenever he got the chance.

Late that evening, Frank arrived home in a dark green Morris van with "O'Hare Racing of Brooklands" painted on each side.

He had been building up the courage to face his wife on the drive home.

"I'm planning to move the engine building business down to Brooklands, but I will come home at weekends," he announced to Margaret as he walked in to the kitchen. "Pete can look after the garage up here while I'm away."

"I bet you don't come back at the weekends," said Margaret angrily. "They race at that nasty place all the time."

"If that's the case, I will come back in the week," Frank replied defensively. Anyway, I'll only be away during the racing season."

"That lasts at least six months," Margaret sighed and pointed out, "And how the Hell will you have any time to come back if you have all those bloody engines to build?"

Before Frank had time to answer, Margaret added:

"I'm going to bed. You can sleep out here on the sofa."

Frank listened as the church clock struck three. Lying, unable to sleep on the uncomfortable lumpy sofa, he felt guilty that he felt so excited. *I have a wife and three lovely girls; why can't I be happy with just them?* he pondered.

Of course, he knew the answer. Family life had never been quite enough for him - he needed more. With a surge of enthusiasm building inside him, he accepted that the racing drug was forcing him away from home again.

171

hadn't dared mention the fact that he had agreed to act as riding mechanic for Freddie at the following weekend's Brooklands Double Twelve race.

The cockerels were crowing the following day as Frank packed a few clothes into his scruffy, old, brown leather bag, ready to leave.

"Take me with you, take me with you," cried nine-year-old Mary, clinging to his better leg as Frank tried to escape. Frank picked her up and gave her a big hug.

"I would love to take you, dear girl, but you must stay here, attend school and learn new things. In a few years, you will be old enough to come everywhere with me…then you will be my right-hand man."

This was a long-running joke between them.

"I'm a girl; you know I'm a girl! I'm going to be your right-hand girl," Mary reminded him.

"Promise I'll get the boys to bring you down on some weekends," said Frank as he got into the driving seat of the Morris. Pete Betts had arrived to open the garage; he stood with Mary as Frank drove away.

Once again, Margaret refused to see Frank off; she remained in the kitchen. In fact, she hadn't spoken to him since their argument the previous night.

Frank's new workshop and semi-permanent home was set up in one of the many sheds that had sprung up in the lower paddock area inside the Brooklands track. The workshop was long enough for three cars, and it had a large wooden workbench running down the left-hand wall.

There's plenty of room to build my engines, thought Frank. Along the back was a partitioned room large enough for a small single bed. It had an old sink and a foldaway table with two chairs to eat at. This was where Frank would spend many of his nights in the future.

The 1930 Brooklands Double Twelve race attracted 51 starters. Frank was to act as Freddie's riding mechanic in his black and silver Brooklands Riley.

"This is bloody great int it Flying Freddie and Fearless Frank back together again," Freddie said with a wide grin as he took a final drag on his Woodbine. Frank wasn't so sure as they joined lined up on the grid for the start.

As he squeezed himself into the Riley's bucket like, hard passenger seat, he clearly remembered the last time he had partnered with Freddie at Spa.

All senses were overwhelmed. Deafening noise from fifty-one powerful engines hurt ears, oily smoke from hot exhausts stung eyes, and clawing burning rubber fumes invaded nose and throat.

The spectacular mass start saw the jostling pack of angry cars surge towards the first right-hand bend, taking them onto the wide, steep banking. Freddie started quickly, mixing with the big boys as the mass of cars roared onto the banking. On reaching full speed, the Riley's 1.5-litre engine was no match for their powerful 3 and 4-litre engines. But it was a handicap race, and Freddie had worked out the lap times he wanted to attain.

They soon settled into a consistent pace. The race was going well; after the second hour, the Riley was in 8th place. Frank found the job of riding mechanic much more enjoyable than his previous experience as a sidecar passenger. Because the cars had no mirrors, his main job in the race was to warn Freddie of any faster Bentleys, Lagondas and Alfa Romeos coming up behind them.

Their engine roar and the wind's whoosh made hand signals the only possible form of communication. Frank would tap Freddie on the shoulder when a Bentley or Alfa approached, travelling 40mph faster than their maximum 100mph.

Then it started to rain. It was just a light shower, so it made little difference to the track surface. Freddie continued to drive flat out. As most drivers became more cautious, the Riley became the fastest car on the track. Within an hour the track dried again, and Frank resumed his observation duties. Five hours of racing passed, and Frank was becoming worried. His body began to feel the effects of the constant pounding it received as the Riley landed each lap after being launched by the two large bumps around the rough Byfleet Banking.

Christ, he thought. *There are another seven hours today and twelve hours tomorrow. I'm not going to be able to manage this.*

Every muscle in his body hurt, and his damaged right knee sent sharp, needle-like pains up his leg every time the car landed. Freddie seemed oblivious and happily continued to drive flat out. The only way he knew.

When we stop again for fuel in two laps, I must tell him I can't carry on; Frank had decided. Then fate took over.

Frank wasn't the only one suffering from the rough track. The Riley was also taking quite a beating. They were halfway around the Byfleet Banking when the weld connecting the left-hand front mudguard support to the body cried 'enough'.

It broke, and the flapping mudguard, caught by the 100mph wind, was ripped from the car. It flew back, catching Frank on the side of the head as it passed and knocking him senseless. Freddie quickly slowed the Riley and steered down to the base of the banking. He drove slowly back to the pits, looking at his friend slumped next to him with concern.

Coasting to a stop at his pit, he screamed at the mechanics,

"Get Frank out of the car, I think he's dead."

They lifted Frank carefully out and laid him on the pit counter. A crimson stream of blood flowed down his cheek, dripping onto his once white overalls to mix with the black oil stains. Distraught, Freddie wandered away, muttering to everyone he bumped into.

"I've killed my best friend. Frank's dead and it's my fault."

A Red Cross nurse arrived at the pits and removed Frank's split helmet. She could see a six-inch slash along his skull, just above his ear. She was gently bathing it when, with a start, Frank came to.

"What happened ... where am I?" he asked, trying to get up.

"Lie still," said the nurse sharply.

"You've had a heavy blow to your head."
Noticing the movement from his friend, Freddie rushed back to the pits.

"Bloody hell, Fearless, I thought you were dead," he said. "But it looks like they have stopped the race. There has been a big accident."

"What race?" replied Frank. He was still unable to understand where he was.

"I think one of the Bentleys has crashed. All of the cars are coming into the pits," Freddie explained.

After the Riley mudguard hit Frank, it had bounced along the track, up into the path of the Bentley being driven flat out by Alexander Dumar. The Le Man winning driver was also a recent ex-lover of Silvia Marshall.

Travelling at 120mph, Dumar had turned the large wooden Bentley steering wheel sharply to the right attempting to miss the lump of Riley metal hurtling towards him, the car was already high on the banking. It's right front wheel ran off the track's top lip, which flipped the Bentley over, ejecting the unfortunate Dumar and his riding mechanic, Wilfred Owens.
The great, green Bentley slid, still upside down, to a smoking, metal-screaming stop and wedged at the top of the Byfleet Banking, with the front half pointing skyward and the tail resting on the track.

The two unfortunate men were thrown over the top lip of the track. They plummeted thirty feet down through the branches of the sturdy fir trees, falling like demented balls on a pinball machine. Both died instantly. Back in the Paddock, Frank had been carried to the first aid hut. With his head bandaged, he tried to leave, but the doctor said, "Hold on, Mr. Cartland, you have suffered a concussion and need to rest."

"I feel fine, I'm off home," said Frank.

The race was abandoned for the day, to be continued the following day.

Freddie immediately retired his car, and Peter Betts, who had attended as the team's assistant mechanic, drove a very groggy Frank home to Cambridgeshire.

"What the hell have you done this time?" was Margaret's reaction when she saw his bandaged head and white face. Mary burst into tears.

"Just leave me in peace," said Frank. "I've had a small bump on the head, and I'm going to bed to rest." As he went into their bedroom, he slammed the door.

Margaret questioned poor Pete mercilessly, but to his credit, he didn't give his boss away, saying that although he hadn't seen what had happened, he'd been told that a piece of metal had fallen on Frank's head.

For two days, Frank suffered headaches and felt dizzy, but by the end of the week, he had recovered sufficiently to be on his way back to his Brooklands shed. Margaret never did find out the real cause of his head injury.

Frank Cartland's reputation continued to grow. Once established at Brooklands, he became known as the leading engine tuner of smaller-engine cars and motorcycles. With Frank's engines, Freddie O'Hare was the man to beat, and he won many races at the track. All the other drivers were desperate to get their engines built by Frank. Silvia Marshall was one of those drivers.

When Silvia first approached him, Frank was preparing to start his Morris van to begin a rare trip home.

Frank, a man of typical desires, couldn't help but feel a surge of intense attraction upon laying eyes on the captivating Silvia who suddenly appeared walking towards him dressed in the immaculate figure-hugging Cambridge blue, racing suit that she and Hellen had specially designed. The top three buttons of the light blue overall were open. Silvia was aware of her effect on men and had mastered the art of using it to her advantage. Frank wound down the driver's door window as she reach the van. Leaning in through the open window she displayed ample cleavage. She said, looking Frank directly in the eye.

"I would do almost anything to try one of your engines in my car Frank, everyone says you have magic in your fingers.

"And I would love to give you one," said Frank without thinking and trying not to look at the display of flesh.

"I'm sure you would!" Sylvia laughed.

"Sor ... sorry, Mrs Marshall," said Frank, embarrassed.

"I didn't mean it like that."

"Call me Silvia," she replied, giving him a wide smile.

This was the first time Frank's path had crossed with any member of the Marshall family.

Little did Frank know, this seemingly innocuous, although certainly memorable, encounter with Mrs Silvia Marshall was a path he would soon come to regret crossing.

Chapter Eighteen

The later years of the 1920s were not kind to George Marshall. He was entirely overshadowed by his wife, both in popularity and in driving skills. George spent most of his time in London nightclubs. His favourite haunt was the Astor Club in Berkley Square, where he lavished money on the beautiful young ladies who frequented it.

After their visit to Le Mans, he fell in with the Bentley boys. They did everything to excess, and he was delighted to be invited to join them. George had always been slightly overweight, but now, eating and drinking constantly, he was piling on the pounds. He was generally unfit, and his fine, blond hair was growing thin. Silvia, despite her faults, still found time to devote to their children. Their son William, whose birth had consolidated her position in the Marshall family, was her pride and joy.

It certainly helped that each child had their own nanny. They spent most of their time at Sefton Manor at the insistence of Lady Victoria. With the nannies and twenty servants to help, Silvia was often accessible to pursue her joint passions of motorsport and handsome young men.

While at the London clubs, George was delighted to meet Hellen Dupery once again. Since their Le Mans meeting, he had thought of her every time he made love. Now, here she was performing in London and looking as beautiful as ever.

Hellen's appearance in London was no accident. She knew her dancing days were ending, and her future would be bleak unless she found herself a wealthy husband—or, failing that, a rich lover.

In France, she had enjoyed a long affair with one of the younger sons of the famous automobile designer and manufacturer, Ettore Bugatti. However, with her uncertain background and current profession, the family had pressured their boy to end the relationship. This had persuaded Hellen to try her luck in London.

While performing her famous fan dance at the Astor Club, she noticed George in the audience. When her act had finished to huge applause and ignoring all the calls from other men for her attention, she quickly went over to his table. Picking up and, in one gulp, swallowing his glass of champagne, she purred, sitting close to him.

"It is so lovely to see you again, George." George greedily sucked in the scent of jasmine from the sensual Shalimar perfume on Hellen's near-naked body. The shine of her skin resembled the glow of a full moon. Her short, blond hair shone, and her deep blue eyes swallowed his soul.

Unusually eloquent and confident, George said breathlessly,

"Oh, Hellen, I have thought about you endlessly since we first met in France. I have wanted to be with you desperately since that moment."

Hellen, who had been anticipating a reaction like this from George, said,

"Oh, George, I have also thought about you often since our meeting at Le Mans."

George, of course, did not pick up the lack of conviction in her voice. Henry Duller, a member of the Bentley Boys, appeared at the table.

"Why, it's Miss Dupery," he said. "It is lovely to see you in England."

George felt nervous. Henry Duller was still very handsome. He had known Hellen and, of course, George's wife, Silvia, for some time.

"I hope you are going to join me for dinner this evening when you finish here?" said Henry, without looking at George.

"Sorry, Henry, Hellen is coming for dinner with me," said George boldly. Hellen gave him one of her special smiles, which seemed to say, "I'm all yours".

George and Hellen started a passionate affair that night. For the first time since his wedding night and honeymoon, sex was exciting and fun for George.

George knew that Hellen also had a strong desire for racing. Still, he didn't realise she had persuaded her lover to loan her one of the family's beautiful blue cars in France.

Over the previous two years, Hellen had proven herself a competent racing driver, winning many minor races in France while driving Hispano-Suiza cars loaned by various wealthy admirers.

Always looking for good advertising opportunities for his cars, Bugatti sent Hellen to Montlhery, a high-speed, banked track on the outskirts of Paris.
The French had designed Montlhery after witnessing the success of Brooklands in England. It was just as fast and just as dangerous.

Bugatti's plan was for Hellen to try breaking the women's land speed record, and she bravely agreed. Many thought he really expected, or hoped, she would kill herself in this attempt. Getting this woman out of his son's life for good had become a priority for Ettior. The date chosen for this attempt was early January, in exceedingly tricky cold and icy conditions.

"Votre fou, tu vas te tuer (You are mad, you'll kill yourself), said Hellen's best friend, a fellow review dancer Maria Lemick.

"Ne vous inquiétez pas pour moi, ceci est ma grande chance d'être un automobilist de course (Don't worry about me; this is my great chance to be a racing motorist.) Hellen replied.

Outwardly, she appeared full of confidence, but inwardly, she was terrified.

Waiting for the signal to start, shivering and nervously tapping the wood-rimmed steering wheel, her slim figure, dressed in clean white overalls, a white linen helmet and a red scarf that flapped in the swirling wind. Hellen's appearance contrasted sharply with the lead grey winter sky.

The signal came. Hellen, with the car already in first gear, released the clutch, pressed her right foot hard on the throttle, and with the rear wheels spinning. Instantly nerves were now forgotten as she became at one with the beautiful blue machine, the roar of the engine, the gusts of the wind, and the pure delight of the drive. It was not just the thrill of racing that drove her, but also the desire to prove herself in a field dominated by men, a challenge she faced with unwavering determination.
For lap after lap, the Bugatti hurtled around the lip of the high, concrete bowl as the engine screamed with joy, and Hellen danced the little car over the vast, wide track.

A huddle of twenty assorted Bugatti officials, timekeepers, mechanics, and pressmen watched from far below her, sheltering in the sparse stone Montlhery pits.

Alongside them, in a heavy overcoat and hat, Ettior Bugatti also observed her progress.

"Eh bien, je dois admettre que, cette fille a du cran "

(Well, I must admit, this girl has guts) he commented to the pressmen.

Hellen kept her speed and concentration, the wind's icy fingers clawing at her cheeks as they rushed past, her shoulders aching as she held the blue machine on the high line of the steep banking. Finally, a signal from the pits told her to stop.

On the slow lap back to the pits, Hellen was disappointed that the run was over. She doubted if she would be able to experience this unique, intense pleasure - a jumbled mixture of excitement, fear, and happiness - ever again. Her emotional journey was a rollercoaster, and despite her euphoria, she was convinced she was not fast enough to break the record.

But the looks on the faces of her lover, Jean Bugatti, the mechanics and the press as she stopped and put the Bugatti engine to sleep quickly dispelled her fears.

Hellen was now the fastest woman in the world, having reached more than 197mph. For a moment, she was still annoyed with herself. 200mph *would have sounded much better,* she thought. Ettior Bugatti had not stayed to congratulate her.

The Montlhery success confirmed Hellen's growing reputation in France as a star automobile driver and celebrated dancer. Her achievements in both fields, a testament to her versatility and talent, had earned her a place in the hearts of the French public.

Upon moving to London, she had managed to

bring a Bugatti Type 35 with her. The car, a symbol of her success and defiance, had been given to her by Ettore Bugatti, as a final bribe. Desperately hoping to drive her away from the Bugatti family for good.

When she arrived in England, Hellen had gone straight to Brooklands. Frank Cartland's reputation for preparing racing cars had already reached French motorsport. Frank's workshop was her target.

All spanners were dropped when this slim, smiling, stunning blond woman walked into Frank's shed.

" Je voudrais parler à Monsieur Frank Cartland .S'il te plaît " Hellen announced to the three-open-mouthed mechanics standing before her.

"Bonjour Mademoiselle," said Frank, walking towards her. "Je sues Frank Cartland."

Frank's two apprentice mechanics were impressed. They had never heard their boss speak French before.

"Bonjour, Frank. Then changing to English she said.

" My name is Hellen Dupery. I have an old car outside, and I would like you to run it for me at Brooklands."

Following Hellen out of the workshop, Frank was faced with an old trailer hitched to an equally old Citroen, but on the trailer…a vision. There sat a muddy and well used blue, 1927 Bugatti Type 35 racing car.

Despite the Bugatti's appearance, Frank's excitement was evident.

"Oh, Miss Dupery, it would be a great pleasure to work on this beauty," he said. Smiling, he ran his hand gently over the swooping curve of the Bugatti's heaven blue tail.

"Excellent, Frank...please call me Hellen. How much money do you want from me to prepare Bleu Bebe?"

Hellen gave Frank one of her broad, seducing smiles as she spoke.

"What's Bleu Bebe?" asked Frank.

"It's my name for this Bugatti; she's my baby," said Hellen.

"Let's not worry about the cost now, er...Hellen, we will get the Bugatti into the workshop. The boys can clean it up, and I'll take a look at the engine."

Hellen had expected the Bugatti to have this effect on Frank. In fact, she was banking on it. She had arrived in England almost penniless.

Entrusting the Bugatti into Frank Cartland's care, Hellen went straight up to London, where she bumped into George Marshall again. With her meeting with Frank and her seduction of George, Hellen's move to England was already going better than she could have hoped. Before long, Hellen was making a name for herself and Bleu Bebe at Brooklands. The pretty, blue Bugatti proved to be very quick and competitive in her skilful hands.

The motoring press wasted no time inventing a strong rivalry between Silvia and Hellen. These two beautiful and fast ladies quickly became headline news. All the newspapers built up the story that George Marshall's wife and his lover were competing for him on and off the racetrack.

In fact, Silvia and Hellen liked each other. They had very similar personalities and laughed a lot at the situation, much to George's discomfort.

Both also enjoyed the intermit pleasures of other women and were mutually attracted to each other. Having already enjoyed each other's company the girls decided to have some fun at George's expense.

Hellen informed Silvia that George planned to take her to the Ritz for dinner, to be followed by a night of passion. Hellen told her their room number, and they agreed that Silvia enter the hotel room using a spare key at exactly 10 p.m. Hellen would make sure that she and George were naked in bed at that time.

The night arrived, and all went to plan. George and Hellen had feasted on oysters and champagne. They were very merry as they started to make love. Meanwhile, Silvia crept into the room and feigned shock at seeing her husband with her friend.

"Oh, George, how could you do this to me!" she exclaimed. Momentarily perturbed, George looked startled, like a rabbit trapped in headlights. Then Hellen said, laughing,

"Hello, Silvia, why don't you join us?" Silvia stripped off her clothes without hesitation and jumped onto the bed with them.

In shock, but quickly realising he had been set up, George watched as the two women immediately began passionately kissing. They quickly moved on, caressing each other, ignoring George they took up Silvia's favourite sixty-nine position soon they were groaning with pleasure as they delighted each other. George took his own enjoyment as he witnessed the erotic actions

It was, he later decided in less happy times, one of the best nights of his life.

Unfortunately, George's life wasn't always going to be this enjoyable. The girls continually goaded him about his lack of racing success. All their racing driver friends had achieved the coveted Brooklands 120mph record badge. This was awarded to all drivers who could average this high speed continuously over three laps of the Brooklands complete circuit. The colourful metal, enamelled badge was proudly carried on all their road going Bentleys and Lagondas.

"Oh, Georgie, come and look. There is no 120mph Brooklands badge on the front of your car. Has someone stolen it?" This became a regular joke between the two women in George's life.

Chapter Nineteen

Silvia had started racing at Brooklands in 1927, the first year the Brooklands Automobile Racing Cub (BARC), reluctantly, allowed women to race against men. Using modified sports cars borrowed from her many male admires she immediately became successful in small handicap races.

"We need a much faster car of our own now." She told George. They had just watched Hellen beating all the men in a scratch race. "If you are ever going to get that badge you need to be able drive more powerful cars."

"Don't expect father will release enough money to allow me to buy a new racing car." Replied a worried looking George.

Exasperated, Silvia said.

"Don't need your bloody family money. I will buy a car myself." Was her angry response.

For the 1931 season, Silvia bought a new car on Freddie O'Hare's recommendation. The car was a dark green Frazer Nash. After their previous conversation, Silvia visited Frank Cartland's workshop again, this time with a large wad of cash.

Walking through the open door of his workshop, she found him with his head deep under the bonnet of a customer's MG.

"Hello again, Frank. Are you ready to give me one now?" she said, waving the cash.
Frank straightened up with a start and banged his head on the edge of the MG's bonnet. Rubbing his head he replied.

"Ah, Mrs. Marshall, er Silvia. Wh....what can I do for you?"

"I want you to re-build the engine of the new

Frazer-Nash, Freddie suggested I buy. Whatever it takes, I want you to give me your best one," Silva said

After their first encounter, Frank was careful with his reply. Still rubbing his sore head, he said,

"I always build all my engines with love and care. I will, of course, do the same for yours."

Silvia moved close to Frank and, teasing him she took his hand in hers, she said

"I can see that you have sensitive and strong fingers, so I'm sure you will give me a good one. I'll get one of the boys to drop the car in tomorrow." Silvia Marshall scattered a wad of cash on the leather driver's seat of the MG.

Red-faced and embarrassed again, Frank muttered,

"I'll do my best for you Mrs. Marshall," as he watched his visitor's shapely figure disappear from his workshop.

The first race Silvia competed in with the new engine was a 4-lap handicap, which she easily won. That victory assured her that the handicap committee would give extremely hard time in any future races, but this didn't worry her.

Silvia had already decided that she and her good friend Hellen Dupery would enter the Frazer Nash for the Brooklands Double Twelve, the hardest and most prestigious race of the year.

The Double Twelve was a thousand-mile race run over two days, with five hundred miles to cover daily. Most people, including her husband George, thought she was mad.

"No woman will be strong enough or can concentrate long enough to win that race," George complained to his mother.

"Well, you should be a man and stop her then," said Victoria Marshall dismissively. Victoria had given up trying to understand her daughter-in-law many years ago. Now, she had as little to do with her as possible. Experience had taught her that she couldn't manipulate Silvia the way she could influence her son.

She also knew that George would not stop Silvia from doing anything if she had decided to do it. Victoria had not allowed envy of other women to affected her until she witnessed Silva's obvious enjoyment of life. She had never allowed herself that luxury. Now she began to realise how she had sacrificed her own pleasures by always putting the Marshall family honor first.

Frank Cartland and Freddie O'Hare thought it was an excellent idea for the girls to share driving the Frazer Nash in the Double Twelve race.

"Just think of the publicity when they win the Brooklands Double Twelve?" an ever-optimistic Freddie said to Frank.

"With my brilliant car preparation and your bloody engine, the girls can't lose."

The Brooklands Double Twelve was held on the 24th and 25th of May. The large prize fund attracted an entry of thirty seven cars. These included 6-litre Bentleys, 3-litre Talbots, 2-litre Lagondas, 1.5-litre Alfa Romeos, Lea Francis, Aston Martins and Frazer Nash, down to the 1,000cc cars, which included the Riley of Silvia Marshall and Hellen Dupery.

The thunderous noise as the race started soon became a steady drone as the thirty-seven cars spread out around the track. The race continued without major incident, and towards the end of the first day, as 500 miles approached, the Frazer Nash was lapping strongly, both girls driving fast but steadily at their agreed-upon pace.

Then disaster struck the race. Two of the green Talbot cars were racing close together when they collided. This was just after they had overtaken Hellen, who had taken over the driving the Frazer-Nash.

One Talbot reared into the air, and Hellen swerved, missing the big green car by inches. The Nash went into a slide, but with tremendous skill Hellen instinctively corrected the skid, regained control, and continued onto the banking for another lap.

Behind her, the Talbot driver lost complete control of his car, which careered into the public enclosure opposite the pits. The hapless driver, Colin Marsh, was thrown out of the Talbot. To the crowd's horror, he was impaled on the spiked railing bordering

the track and killed instantly. Meanwhile, the driverless Talbot ran on into the crowd crushing three spectators.
Tragically they were also killed.

Sensational headlines in the London papers that night demanded that the race be stopped.

"You must retire now," said a red-faced George Marshall as he had subdued dinner with Silvia and Hellen that evening.

"I forbid you to carry on with this madness. One of you could get killed."

The girls were unusually quiet. But though shaken by the incident and tired after 500 miles of racing, they were determined to continue.

"It's so sweet of you, Georgie, but we are big girls now. We can take care of ourselves," said Silvia.

"We have had our close shave in this race, so tomorrow will be fine," added Hellen.
They had every intention of being on the starting grid the following morning.

Despite the paper's headlines the race continued the next day as planned.

The day dawned bright and clear, and all the drivers soon forgot about the previous day's dramas. The little green Nash roared around the concrete bowl.

"That engine is purring like a contented cat." Freddie shouted across the pits to Frank as the Nash passed them to complete another lap of the track. Silva and Hellen were driving fast but taking no risks, while most of the other, bigger cars were experiencing trouble, with engines misfiring, punctures, and a few accidents.

Fortunately, no accidents were severe, and there were no more injuries.

Both ladies were hot, dirty and tired. Streaks of oil and black tyre dust covered their light blue overalls and their faces. When the chequered flag waved to signal the end of the race all hardships were forgotten. Silvia and Hellen were ecstatic. Just finishing this brutal and punishing race had been a tremendous achievement.

After the endless high-pitched sounds of screaming engines and sliding tyres, the sudden silence was palpable Everyone left with ringing sounds in their ears as they waited for the loudspeakers to announce the results. When the speakers crackled into life, the girls jumped around and shouted with delight. They had finished 4th overall behind three Talbots.

With everyone congratulating them on their success, a further announcement began. Everyone stopped to listen.

"Here are the results after the handicap calculations have been made. The winners are Silvia Marshall and Hellen Dupery with their Frazer-Nash averaging 84.41mph. "

Everyone around the pits went wild with delight drowning out the rest of the announcement. Silvia and Hellen thoroughly deserved their win.
Before the event, the handicap committee had spent hours calculating and setting the handicap for each car.

That evening, now clean the glamorous girls accepted the magnificent Double Twelve Trophy at the prize-giving dinner. Champagne flowed all night in the Brooklands clubhouse, although George had gone home to bed alone. The girls continued their celebrations together.

Chapter Twenty

By 1933, George had become fed up with being the butt of his famous wife, and his equally famous lover's jokes. The final straw had been as he listened to his old schoolmate, Allister McApline, boasting in the Brooklands clubhouse after he got his 120mph badge.

"Remember all those years ago, George, back at Leamington School? he had said loudly.

"We both said we would be racing at Brooklands, and I told you I would beat you. Don't suppose you will ever get a 120mph badge George."

"I will have mine before this season is over." Was his angry response.

How hard can it be to keep your foot flat down for a few laps? He thought.

George had decided that he had no choice. It was time he had some motor racing glory for himself. Knowing he didn't have the skill to win any major races getting the badge was his best option. To achieve he would need a powerful car suitable to help him obtain that coveted 120mph badge. But that would be expensive.

" I decided I will need a new car to get my badge." he confided to Silvia. "I would like to buy one of the old Le Mans-winning Bentleys and develop it, but it's going to be very expensive."

"Why don't you ask your parents to forward some of your inheritance. If they think you are upholding Marshall honor, doing it for you family glory. It would be like going into battle like your famous ancestor Sir William."

Silvia had replied, more as a joke and thinking: *He will never have the guts to do that.*

She was pleasantly surprised that for once George proved her wrong. With some reluctance Victoria and her husband agreed to the idea. The car would be named "Crusader". So, George was able to go to W.O Bentley with the cash.

Once his mechanics had rebuilt the car George had the name Marshall Crusader sign written on it vast bonnet. The mighty machine was painted deep red, with the Marshall coat of arms on both sides of the bonnet.

Everyone told George he should have the special 4.5-litre supercharged engine rebuilt by Frank Cartland, so George went to Frank's workshop at Brooklands. Although George knew Frank had been building his wife's engines and looking after his lover's Bugatti, he had deliberately avoided talking to Frank in the past.

I certainly have nothing in common with him, he thought to himself.

In fact, meeting at Brooklands was not the first time Frank and George had seen each other, although neither of them remembered the occasion.

This had been at Newmarket Racecourse when Frank was ten, and George was just eight.
Joe had taken Frank to the Newmarket races, as he often did in those days. They had walked the three miles from Burlham along the Devil's Dyke to the racecourse. Between races, they would play, racing up and down the steep banks of the dyke and tumbling into the ditch.

When the horses came out of the paddock, they would run to the start and watch the magnificent thoroughbred horses and their colourful jockeys' line up behind the starting tapes. Frank loved the start drama, with each jockey straining and pushing their great mounts into the best positions. Then, the tapes would go up with a sharp, whip-like snapping sound.

Sometimes, they would run to the rail outside the track and crane their necks to glimpse the race's finish as the horses charged past. Resting from their play, Frank and Joe leant on the rail and looked across the track to the enclosures where the rich, well-dressed, paying spectators were.

Peering back at them and standing all by himself, a sad little blond boy was dressed in a tweed suit with a tie and a waistcoat.

"Look at that poor little sod, he must be boiling dressed like that," said Joe.

"I'm glad I've only got on a vest and shorts," Frank had said. Then they had run back to play on the bank.

George was hot and very bored; he hated horse racing. Most of the time his father spent at the bar drinking, then giving money to a man standing on a box shouting out strange numbers.

He had wished he could be like that scruffy little boy on the other side of the racecourse, running about free and happy.

Frank was refitting a freshly rebuilt engine into Hellen Dupery's Bugatti when George Marshall marched into the workshop. He had his three mechanics close behind.

"Cartland, I want you to stop whatever you are doing and start work on rebuilding my new engine." Frank slowly turned to look directly at George and said, "Good afternoon to you, too, Mr. Marshall." Then he put his head back under the bonnet of the Bugatti. Like most

of the racing community, Frank deliberately didn't address George as "the Honorable".
George continued.

"My men here can have the engine with you tomorrow. I will expect it back, rebuilt to the highest standard in two weeks."

With a deep sigh, Frank stood up and looked straight at George.

"If I agree to rebuild your engine, Mr. Marshall, you must agree to run it as I say. And you will get it back when I think it's ready, not before."

George was taken aback. He wasn't used to being spoken to like that. Usually, working people just did what he told them to do without question.

"Er, very well. We have a deal," said George. "Send your bill to my estate manager when the engine is ready." Then he turned and walked out of the workshop, his men following in line close behind.

Stupid sod hasn't even asked the price. Thought Frank

Silvia and Hellen had had a thrilling race six weeks before the meeting in which George planned to reach the 120mph lap. Silvia beat Hellen for the first time, winning by just one car's length. The engine she used had been specially rebuilt that week by Frank Cartland.

Silvia was extremely happy that evening after drinking a celebratory bottle of champagne to toast her victory. When the party broke up she decided it was time to thank Frank for his skills.

We gave him a small share of the prize money after the Double Twelve victory last year. The clever little man deserves a special prize this time, Giggling to herself. *I will give him something better than money to remember this victory.*

Frank sat alone in his workshop, resting after the hectic day. Quietly smoking a final Woodbine, he was thinking of going home. There was a soft squeak from the old hinges as his workshop door opened. He turned at the sound and watched, to his great surprise, as Silvia Marshall tottered in.

"I've got a present for you, Frankie," she said, weaving her way, a little unsteadily, between the still warm metal of her winning Riley and Hellen's beautiful Bugatti.

"It's to say thank you for building me such wonderful engines."

Frank noticed she was wearing high-heeled black shoes and an oversized golden fox fur coat. *It must be a bit hot to be wearing a coat like that,* he thought.

Silvia stopped in front of Hellen's Bugatti, only six feet from Frank. Then she turned to face him and opened the golden coat revealing her stunning and gleaming naked body. Frank shot out of his seat as if he had received an electric shock.

"Come and get your present, Frankie," she said, in little more than a demure whisper.

Frank was speechless, he couldn't take his eyes off her body.

Since his night with Susan in the Isle of Man, Frank hadn't been unfaithful to Margaret. Being surrounded by girls and women at home gave him respect for them, which meant that, even when sex was offered to him, he was able to resist it. But this was different. No emotion was involved. Frank had no time for any thoughts of guilt. This was pure lust.

Throwing away his half-smoked Woodbine, he walked right up to Silvia and accepted the invitation, immediately cupping her pendulous breasts in his, still oily, hands. He breathed in the sensual fragrance of her Chanel perfume as, smiling, she pushed him away slightly and arched her back over the lovely, curved, warm tail of Hellen's blue Bugatti. Sliding both her hands into a gap in Frank's overalls she pulled hard, ripping them apart. The overalls steel buttons burst off, flying across the workshop floor, one pinging off the blue paintwork of the Bugatti.

"I hope that didn't scratch the paintwork, my lady," said Frank with a wide smile.

In one swift movement, Silvia dragged aside his pants, and his already-erect penis sprung out from the gaping overalls.

"My, Frankie, you are not tall, but you sure are a big boy."

Frank only had one thought as Silvia grabbed his throbbing member and guided it straight into her. For Frank, with that exquisite sensation came an unusual vision. One of his beloved lightened pistons gliding up and down in the beautifully honed bores of his best engine. Faster and faster went the piston, until the mixture exploded right at the top of the stroke. Silvia let out a strangled scream, and for a moment, nothing but pure pleasure existed for either of them. Coming back to reality, Frank felt a strange dampness spreading down his legs. He looked down and noticed a large wet patch growing on his overalls. He pulled away quickly and stood with a rapidly lowering penis. It was shrinking like a giant slug hit by a sprinkling of salt.

Frank had a look of bewilderment on his face. Seeing Frank's shocked expression, Silvia said, with a deep laugh,

"What's the matter, Frankie? Have you never had a golden shower before? You should be incredibly pleased with yourself. That doesn't happen to me very often."

Unable to speak, Frank watched as Silvia unwrapped herself from the curvaceous, blue tail of the Bugatti.

She gave him a quick peck on the cheek and pulled her fur coat back around her shoulders. "I hope you enjoyed your present, Frank", she whispered in his ear. Then, without a backward glance, Silva walked away and out of the workshop.

Frank knew this hadn't been a dream … his legs were soaking wet.

Frank drove home to his Cambridgeshire village still in shock from the evenings event. By the time he drove back into the yard at Ivy Cottage, it was after midnight. Margaret was already in their bed, asleep. Getting into bed beside her, Frank, still thinking of the surprising event recently experienced, felt himself getting hard. Frank turned towards Margaret and pressed against her warm, soft body. Pulling up her nightdress, he pushed himself between her legs. It had been some months since they had last made love.

"You must have had a good day," Margaret murmured sleepily, welcoming the unexpected attention. Frank soon climaxed deep inside his wife. All the while, he was thinking about Silvia and the unexpected present he had received.

They both turned over, and Margaret went straight back to sleep. Frank lay with his eyes open in the inky darkness of their bedroom. With no moonlight, it was the darkness in which your mind builds its own shapes. With Silvia's visit on his mind, Frank's shapes were the sensuous curves of her spooning with the swooping curves of the blue Bugatti.

Did that really happen to me? He thought. But he knew it had. This time, it was not wood smoke he could smell on his skin; it was the flowery fragrance of Silvia's perfume.

He also knew he could never tell anyone about the day's experiences. He could imagine Freddie's reaction if he told him.

"Bloody hell, fearless, you must have been having one of your weird dreams again—a wet one this time. Silva Marshall wouldn't touch you with a bargepole! "

No…he was sure no one would ever believe him.

Chapter Twenty-one

Six weeks later at the next Brooklands meeting a large crowd turned up to watch the races. The whole Marshall family had also arrived to witness George's attempt to win his 120mph badge.

George managed to persuade his parents, Lord and Lady Marshall, to come along to support him. They had, with reluctance, agreed. Silvia brought their 10-yearold son, William, to experience his first motor race. William had recently been taken by his grandmother for his initiation at the tomb of his ancient ancestor.

"I can understand why this ceremony seems so important to you, grandmother," he had said to Victoria as she led him out of the Templar Chapel. His stone kiss and bloodletting on the tomb of Sir William Marshall completed.

"I have great respect for the family history, but to me, just being a Marshall will be enough to ensure that I respect the family name."

Before the trip, his mother had told him how his father had been frightened when he had been taken for his initiation.

"The whole tradition is out of date. It's stupid," Silvia had said to him. William, even at ten years old, had his own ideas. He had never been close to his father, who didn't seem to be able to talk to him as a father should. He thought; *most of the time, I feel more grown-up than he appears to be.*

"I'll do it just to keep grandmother happy." William had told Silvia.

William was looking forward to the trip to Brooklands. Interested to find out why this place seemed to play such an important place in his parents' lives. He did look forward to boasting to his school chums about his father's racing success.

Around 10am on the morning of the record attempt, George entered Frank's workshop with his family and hangers-on. He was keen to show off his new racing car. An excited William ran up to the gleaming, red machine and went to jump into the seat.

"Don't touch it!" shouted his father sharply, halting William in his tracks. Feeling embarrassed and disappointed, William stood beside the large, brown leather seat while everyone stared at him.
Already tucked into the corner of the driving seat sat Bertie, his father's scruffy, old brown bear. William felt a pang of jealousy. *He thinks more of that scruffy old bear than he does of me,* he thought.

The awkward silence of the moment was broken as Frank appeared from the back of his workshop after hearing all the noise.

"Ah, everyone, this is my man, Cartland," George announced to his entourage.

"He has rebuilt the wonderful new engine in the Marshall Crusader to my specification." Frank ignored him and gave William a knowing smile as he walked past to get a spare set of spark plugs from his workbench. George continued showing off his car to the party.

Frank had been really looking forward to this subsequent encounter with Silvia. He'd caught a glimpse of her as he walked across the workshop. She looked sensational in a low-cut, cherry-red dress, almost the same shade of red as the racing car.

He'd been instantly aroused. Frank, wearing brand-new, sparkling-white overalls, had washed and slicked back his hair. He'd even scraped most of the dirt out from under his fingernails. When she saw him, Silvia, out of the rest of the Marshall family's earshot, said,

"My Goodness, Frank, what have you done to yourself. I preferred you when you were … dirty."

With the viewing finished, the Marshall group filed out of Frank's workshop behind George. Silvia gave Frank a wink as the party went to the clubhouse bar for drinks.

"Make the tea, Cartland, my good man," said a voice from the back of the workshop. Freddie O'Hare had been standing out of sight the whole time while the Marshall group were present.

"Fuck off, Freddie," replied Frank sharply. He was disappointed at Silvia's reaction to seeing him all smartened up.

"Don't worry about that stupid bugger, George Marshall," said Freddie, "it doesn't look like his family like him any more than the rest of us. Tell you what, I'll make the tea."

That did make Frank smile. Freddie's special tea always had a giant slug of cheap brandy.
They stood drinking their special tea as they admired the beautiful, red streamlined Marshall Crusader.

"I think even with my bad leg, I could lap this beauty around Brooklands at 120mph," Frank remarked. "George Marshall should have no trouble." "Don't be so sure, I wouldn't trust that stupid bugger to drive 100 yards without hitting something," was Freddie's reply.

At noon, George went out for his practice run. He did four fast laps but was still almost 5mph slower than his target of 120mph. George quickly drove the car back into the crowded paddock, sliding the rear wheels and spraying the startled spectators with gravel. He slammed on the brakes stopping next to his mechanics and Frank.

Red-faced, he jumped out of the car before raging at Frank.

"Cartland, your bloody engine is no good. It needs more revs," he screamed.

"The engine is fine… it's more likely to be your crap driving," muttered Frank in reply.

George pretended not to hear this. He gave orders to his three mechanics, who were already checking the hot red car.

"Strip down the back axle and get that axle ratio changed so that I can rev this bloody useless engine some more," George shouted at them.

"Hang on, lads, I told your boss that the safety limit for this engine is only for 4000 revs maximum," said a startled Frank.

"You can't let them change the axle ratio. If you do, the engine will likely blow up," he added to George.

The scar on Frank's forehead had turned bright pink.

"It's my bloody car, I'll do what I like with it," an angry George shot back. "And they work for me, so they will do whatever I tell them."

"We had a deal that you would run that engine as I say," said Frank. Then he shrugged his shoulders and added, "but it's your bloody funeral."

Frank turned away and quickly limped back to his shed in disgust. He was drinking a cup of tea and a having a smoke five minutes later when Freddie came rushing in,

"I've just seen one of those Marshall lads swearing about the hot oil burning his sodding hands while he's stripping the back axle on the Crusader. Has something broken?" he asked.

"No, that stupid sod George Marshall has told them to put a higher ratio in so he can use more revs. You know that will make the car easier to drive below its limit, but car was good for one hundred and twenty five easy, with my ratio and a decent bloody driver."

"Fucking fool," was Freddie's simple reply.

Chapter Twenty-two

"Now get ready for the event you have all been waiting for, George Marshall and his magnificent car are going for their 120mph badge."

The excited voice of the Brooklands commentator echoed through the circuit loudspeakers.

George Marshall stepped into the driver's seat to prepare for his record attempting laps after the last race of the day had been run. Looking around at the large crowds, he could see their expectant, excited faces watching his every move. *God, I wish I was anywhere but here. Now my bloody wife is going to cause more trouble.* He watched as Silvia, in her tight red dress approached. She provided a stirring sight for the gathered press and photographers surrounding the car.

To demonstrate her support in front of the press, she gave her husband a final kiss on his lips. But as George pulled on his white leather helmet and lowered his racing goggles, she whispered to him,

"Now's your chance Georgie, show me you aren't the coward I think you are."

I'll show you, bitch were his thoughts as he slammed the car into first gear. *Come on Bertie, we can do this.* He gave his lifelong companion, Bertie bear, tucked down next to him, a final squeeze before flooring the throttle. With a clenched jaw and fixed stare he released the brake and as the rear tyres squealed in protest, he turned the bright-red, flame-spitting Marshall Crusader out onto the vast home straight of the Brooklands track.

Silvia's words reinforced his determination to average the 120mph lap needed for his badge. He would never have admitted it to anyone, but with stomach churning and heart thumping so hard it felt like it would burst out of his chest, George Marshall was lonely and scared.

George knew that on the practice run earlier, he had panicked and lifted his foot off the throttle as the car drifted towards the top of the high Byfleet Banking. He also knew that this was the real reason he hadn't been able to reach top speed - there wasn't any fault in the engine. This time, he thought, he would not lift his right foot whatever happened.

The first lap went well as he built up speed. The engine responded instantly with the extra revs allowed by the axle ratio change. By the second lap's end, the excited circuit announcer shouted the speed.

"119mph, just 1mph to go for George Marshall."
In the cockpit, George, to his amazement, although his body ached from the effort to hold the Crusader high on the rough banking at these high speeds, he felt a growing confidence that he would succeed.   The Marshall Crusader was a streaking flash of red as it roared past the paddock crowds. The high whine of the super-charged engine was evidence to all that George still had the throttle wide open.

Frank had his binoculars trained on the red monster as the car went out onto the Railway Straight for its final, third lap.

"Fuck," he said under his breath. He noticed a tell-tale light trail of smoke from the fish-tale exhaust pipe. He instinctively knew exactly what was happening inside his precious engine. Frank could visualize the pistons pumping up and down inside the engine's bores. Because of the axle change they were now moving faster than they had been designed to do. Frank also knew from the exhaust smoke that some piston rings had broken under the intense strain, and oil was escaping past them into the combustion chamber.

"Be a miracle if it lasts the lap. It's only a matter of time," he muttered to no one in particular.

Lighting another Woodbine, he turned and started slowly walking away from the crowds in the Paddock. He was certain the poor engine would destroy itself unless George lifted his right foot on this lap.

In the car's cockpit, George was oblivious to the drama taking place inside the screaming engine in front of him.

He was pleased with himself. *This will show them all, they will never treat me like a fool after these laps.*

Halfway through the third lap, the tremendous red car had drifted dangerously close to the top lip of the track. However, still, George managed to keep his right foot flat on the floor to hold the throttle pedal wide open, but the revs were rising well above their safety limit.

The force of the wind pushed George's cheeks outward giving his face a manic grin, as the car with supercharger screaming, roared onto the Home Banking. The red monster came into full view of the packed Paddock as it flashed under the Members' Bridge and crossed the white timing line. The last happy thoughts of George were that the lap must have been much better than

120mph. At the same moment the engine, unable to take any more abuse, gave up the struggle and blew apart.

Until that second, all the drama had been happening unseen inside the engine. As Frank expected a poor piston, no longer lubricated by the broken rings, had seized in its bore, but the crankshaft was still turning at more than 4500 revs per minute. The crowd heard the ensuing cannon-like blast as the shaft smashed the connecting rod through the side of the metal cylinder block. Boiling water, steam and hot black oil exploded out onto the track, into the cockpit and over the rear tyres of the stricken car. To the horror of the crowds in the Paddock, the car seemed to magically disappear inside a great cloud of grey-black smoke.

The loud explosion George heard above the sound of the rushing wind was the first he knew of the disaster. Instantly scalding water and oil swamped his body and face, inflicting instant sheering pain. The car's rear end, already on the edge of adhesion, slid up to the right as the hot oil coated the tyres. George intuitively turned up into the skid but the effect of the banking and his steering correction swung the rear of the red car violently back to the left.

"No, no, no, it's not fair…" No one heard his despairing screams as the momentum ejected George violently from his driver's seat high into the air. He was still travelling at over 90mph as he landed headfirst onto the sloping concrete track. His white leather racing helmet offered him no protection as the heavy impact with the unforgiving concrete splitting his skull, like a ripe watermelon dropped onto a hard surface.

The driverless, smoking, stricken car continued backwards down the steep-banked track, gathering speed as it reached the bowl at the bottom of the slope. Horrified, the crowd suddenly realised that the uncontrolled red monster was heading straight for them and, on mass, turned and scattered in all directions with screams and panic.

Rapidly reaching the bottom of the track slope, the driverless Marshall Crusader continued its backward charge at undiminished speed charging the earth banking which protected the parking areas from the track. The bank acting as a launching pad for the car, which hurtled up it, arcing high over the panic-stricken spectators and turning over as it flew through the air. With a large explosion, it landed squarely on top an shinny green Austin 7 motorcar containing the hapless Mr. and Mrs. Smyth, who had been completely unaware of their fate,

While, almost unnoticed, the lifeless body of George Marshall continued its slow slide down from the top of the steep banked track, its progress marked by a snail-like, bright red trail of blood and brains on the stark white concrete.

Mr and Mrs Smyth were attending their first race meeting at Brooklands. They were sitting in Albert Smyth's pride and joy, their new 1933 Austin 7 saloon motorcar.

In fact, their real surname was Smith. Albert's wife, Madge, had persuaded him to change their name when they married.

"It makes us sound more important," she had said to Albert.

The Austin 7 was the first car that Albert had owned. He had been saving for it over the previous two years, putting a little money away each week until he had the £118 needed to buy the car. When he got to the showroom, the salesman persuaded him to spend an extra £10 to get the deluxe saloon with actual leather seats.

Albert proudly drove the small Austin home with great care. His wife Madge didn't share his love for the vehicle, and she was furious that he had spent the extra £10.

"You are a stupid man, Albert Smyth. You knew I wanted that new three-piece suit in Harrison's furniture shop window. Now we can't afford it."

Albert kept quiet and went out to polish his new car. The Smyth's had been invited to the Brooklands race meeting by the manager of the South London garage where Albert had bought his new Austin 7.
Albert had been looking forward to the trip, having dreamt of visiting Brooklands for many years. In the week leading up to the event, his fellow clerks at the bank where he worked joked that they had never seen him so excited about anything.

Disappointingly, the day had been spoilt for him by the constant complaints of his wife. Madge had hated Brooklands from the moment she arrived. They had left home early for the trip, and Albert had found a good spot at the top of the paddock in the spectators' parking area. Madge couldn't understand why anyone would want to come to this vast, dusty, concrete place. It was full of loud, harsh engine noise that hurt her ears and the pungent smell of burnt oil that stung her nose. But worst of all were the awful snobbish crowds, with their posh big cars and superior attitudes.

Madge had bought a new hat for the special day, but the wind blew it off the moment she stepped out of the car. All day, the wind remained too strong for her to wear the hat. She put on her best scarf instead but looking at all the glamorous women in their sharp suits and

Hermes scarves, Madge felt entirely out of place and highly uncomfortable.

All she had wanted today was for Albert to take her on a picnic to their quiet spot by the Thames at Windsor. She hadn't wanted to come to this nasty, smelly, unpleasant place but knew it would please Albert. While making the sandwiches that morning, she looked forward to eating them on a rug in some quite spot, not realising that would be impossible at this place.

Madge was in a terrible mood and would not get out of the car. The couple sat in unhappy silence, eating the last of their fish paste sandwiches. Madge was impatient for the gates to open so they could get away. She was desperate to be home in their quiet, semidetached house in Richmond.

Appetite gone, Madge wound down the car window to throw her last sandwich away.

At least Albert's final thoughts were happy ones. in his own little world as he sat in the driver's seat, imagining what it must be like charging around the track in that big red car. Playing with the advance and retard levers on the Austin's steering wheel he breathed in deeply, and the wonderful, rich leather smell coming from the olive-green seats of his beloved little Austin made him smile. *Oh well*, he thought. *At least I've experienced this magical place.*

By the time the accident happened, Frank had walked halfway back to his workshop. He was intending to pack up and go home, as he anticipated that an angry George Marshall would be towed back in the blown-up car. When the sound of the screams from the crowd reached him, he turned just in time to see the final act of the drama, as the inverted Marshall Crusader crushed the little Austin 7.

He ran back towards the devastation as fast as his ruined knee would let him…and found himself at a scene of carnage. There was nothing he could do.
Suddenly, a jet of hot, rust-colored water spurted from the broken radiator of the steaming mechanical mess. For a split-second, Frank thought. *Looks like it's taking a piss*. Then he noticed, next to the smoking wreck, a pearlwhite arm severed at the elbow. The fingers on the small hand were still clutching a fish paste sandwich.

Others soon arrived, and they all desperately tried to pull the two cars apart, but it was far too late to save Mr. and Mrs. Smyth. Eventually a breakdown truck dragged the Marshall Crusader off the little Austin. Remarkably, most of the visible damage to the big red car was superficial. However, extracting the bodies of Albert and Madge from their flattened Austin 7 was a difficult and traumatic operation.

Mechanics cut the roof off the car with hacksaws and found that Albert's upper body had been crushed down onto the steering wheel.

The violent impact had forced the steering wheel so far into his chest that it couldn't be removed. The wheel had to be cut from the Austin's bent steering column, and poor Albert taken to the mortuary with the wheel still embedded in his chest. The body of Madge, less its left arm, had been compressed down into the passenger side foot-well of the Austin. Most of her bones had been crushed by the impact. Curled into a tiny ball, she looked like a bloody little foetus in the womb.   Mercifully, there were only three fatalities from this disaster.
However, two people broke their legs, and many others

had cuts and bruises sustained in the panic as they fell in the stampede to avoid the stricken car. The Marshall family had been watching the unfolding drama from the advantage of the balcony in the Brooklands clubhouse. Although they were some distance from the crash, they all watched the horrific site of George's body being ejected from the Crusader. It seemed inevitable that the catastrophic accident had killed George.

The reaction of each was interesting. Silvia turned away and gave a soft scream. Then, clutching her stomach, she collapsed into a chair, much to her son William's distress and confusion.

The older Marshalls, John and Victoria, slowly put down their binoculars and remained standing next to each other in silence. They had, of course, experienced the pain of loss before. Now, they had just witnessed, first-hand, the death of their last living son. Victoria's first thought, looking down into the tear-streaked face of her grandson William, was: *Thank God George has had a son.*

William had been extremely excited when they arrived that morning, and he had his first sight of the Brooklands track. Unfortunately, his father's attitude towards him had left him disappointed. He had hoped, and expected, that his father would have at least let him sit in the Crusader. *At least he cant embarrass me anymore* William thought, and immediately felt guilty. George had practically ignored his son all morning and shouted at him in front of all those people.
Now, with the scenes of chaos outside and his family's mixed reactions, he was old enough to know that the future direction of his life had changed forever.

A miserable drizzling rain started in the evening after the last officials left Brooklands. Quickly rain washed the remaining red stain of George's life blood from the small ridges and furrows in the concrete track. Evidence of the tragedy soon erased, and darkness began its relentless creep along the steep banking

Little Bertie who had been tucked safely into the seat next to George had also been violently thrown from the car at the same instant as its owner. The bear sent flying over the top lip of the banked racetrack and into the trees. Here some branches of a large Norway spruce arrested his flight. Bertie hung in that tree suspended by one long arm as if looking down on the catastrophic scene below. He even gave the impression of waving.
 For two years, Bertie remained stuck in the fir tree, unnoticed. The branches slowly grew around him holding the little bear fast in their grip. Then birds discovered him. First, magpies came to peck out Bertie's shiny glass eyes and the metal stud in his ear, then crows and pigeons arrived to steal his straw. The rain, snow and cold eventually rotted his brown furry body, and Bertie completely disappeared.

The rest of the day following the accident became a blur for most of those close to the disaster.
Frank returned to his workshop, packed his tools into the Morris van, and drove sadly and slowly back to his Cambridgeshire home. When he arrived, he suddenly realised he couldn't remember any details of the journey. "That's good. You are back early for once," Margaret commented lightly when he walked into the kitchen. Her mood changed the moment she noticed his ashen face.

"You never get back from that place before midnight. What on earth has happened this time?"   "George Marshall crashed his car. He and some other people have been killed," Frank said. "The engine I built blew up because that stupid bastard over-revved it ...
I'm sure there will be a lot of trouble."

Frank wasn't normally a drinker, but this evening, he went into the front room and poured himself a large glass of whiskey. Margaret stomped in after him.

"Well done! For years, you have been trying to kill yourself. Now, it sounds like you've helped kill someone else. I hope you're satisfied. Bloody engines and racing have finally ruined our lives. You are no better than your murderous brother!"

Frank had the whiskey bottle in his hand, and his instinct to turn and slam it into the side of his wife's face was powerful. A split second before that action, he turned and, not looking at her, pushed past. He went straight to his garage workshop and locked the doors.

Here in his sanctuary, everything was quiet and still. Amid the engines, the smells of burnt oils and the faint aroma of exhaust fumes, which he loved, he could relax. He knew his wife would regret that last remark, and he didn't hate her for it. He had grown to expect her to lash out at him when things went wrong.

Bleu Bebe, the heaven-blue Bugatti, was sitting at the back of the workshop, where Frank had left her when he brought the car up from Brooklands two days earlier. *Two days, seems a lifetime ago*, he thought.

He pulled off the dust sheet covering the car and climbed into the narrow, brown leather bucket shaped driver's seat. Holding the four-spooked, wood-rimmed steering wheel in his right hand, he took a great gulp from the whiskey bottle. He felt the coarse, fiery liquid flowing down his throat and into his stomach. It sent calming signals to his brain, and a second large gulp made him drift away.

I'm rushing downhill past the pits at Spa Francorchamps. Roaring wind and engine noise fill my head. The robust and super-charged engine in the Bugatti Type 35 urges me towards the left-hand bend at the bottom of the hill. The wood-rimmed steering wheel judders, sending shock waves through my hands, arms and shoulders as I turn into the bend. Braking hard, the firm brake pedal gives me confidence as I go down to second gear and slow into the right-hand l'Ancienne Douane hairpin. The back end of the little car kicks out, trying to spin me around. With a quick left flick of the wood-rimmed steering wheel, I am accelerating hard out of the hairpin. Now, I am climbing steeply uphill onto the long straight. Picking up speed, I am drifting through the left-hand sweep at the top of the hill. I start plunging downhill, 4th gear flat out. The rev counter reads 5,300 as I flash past the houses at Burnenvillie and then Malmseys' left and right curves. They are already behind me. 'Get ready,' I tell myself, the Masta kink is ahead. 'Keep your right foot hard down,' my heart says, but my brain says, 'lift it, you stupid bugger'. I ignore that, and phew, made it.. The Bugatti is kicking up dust at the edge of the road. The exhilaration, the rushing wind, the flies peppering my face, the sweet, singing, super-charged engine. I'm on full power down to Stavelot, the tight, right-hand bend. The straight-cut gears engage the second gear as I press the sharp clutch. Braking hard now, I feel the front wheels scrubbing sideways, protesting. I'm through, uphill again, building up speed all the time, gliding, almost floating, through the fast curves of La Carriere, my right foot flat to the floor. The fearsome Blanchimont approaches, and the narrow Bugatti tyres dance sideways as I turn too fast into the first left bend; it's over-steering! But a slight correction and all's well again. I drift gracefully through the second left-hand bend and touch the grass at the road's edge. Flat out to the left-hand kink again, and the La Source hairpin is already upon us! Braking hard, I change to first gear and kiss the grass, with the front right tyre at the apex.

Next door's cockerel bellowed a "cock-a-doodledoo", an early morning announcement of territory. This awoke Frank with a start, momentarily unsure of where he was. Then, the pain in his knee left him in no doubt. He was still wedged in the driver's seat of the Bugatti. On the passenger seat, he noticed an empty bottle of whiskey on its side. The remains of its contents were puddled on the brown leather seat.

Slowly and painfully, he extracted himself from the vehicle and unbolted the workshop door. The dull dawn light and the hard, sharp air made him decide to walk off his aches, pains, and hangover by going to his place, the Devil's Ditch.

An hour later, a refreshed Frank walked back into the yard. He could smell the toast and hear the highpitched noise of his young daughters. They were shouting and laughing as they ate their breakfast in the kitchen and got ready for school. Suddenly, somehow, the future didn't seem quite so bleak.

A swift splash of cold water from the outside pump sharpened him up. Frank walked into the house to face his wife, and another day.

Chapter Twenty-three

The inquest had been set for 20th September, three weeks after the accident. It was to be held at the Coroner's Court in Weybridge.

The day after the accident, once again, journalists commandeered the Red Lion pub with the Cartland family, deemed newsworthy again.

Both Cartland and Foster families refused to speak to any of them. So, they asked constant questions of the neighbors and dragged up all the old sensational stories.

Two days before the inquest, Mary came home from school early.

"What's the matter? Why have you come home?" Margaret asked Mary when she stomped into the house.
"Billy Knowles said that my dad is a killer, just like his brother, so I punched him in the face," said Mary.

"Then that old witch, Miss Manners, sent me home."

"Oh, Mary, you can't go around hitting people. I hope you have said you're sorry?" said Margaret.
"I'm not sorry, I'd hit him again, or anyone else, that said that about my dad," Mary replied.

"Go to your room this minute. I've had enough of all this," Margaret shouted as she pushed her daughter towards the stairs.

Margaret's nerves were shot. Even though Doctor Jones had given her some sedatives, she felt unable to cope with even more stress. Mary stamped up to her room and slammed the door. The moment Frank came in from the workshop, Margaret demanded

"Your daughter has been hitting people at school. I want you to go up there and punish her."

With a sigh Frank climbed the stairs to Mary's room. He knocked softly on the door and went in. The room was empty, and the bedroom window wide open. *The little monkey had shimmied down the drainpipe.* he thought.

Margaret had followed Frank up to the room. She didn't trust him to be firm with their daughter. "Where is she?" she asked, a hysterical pitch to her voice.

"Don't worry, I'll find her," said Frank. "This is all your fault as usual". Frank knew exactly what the following sentence would be. "Your bloody motors will be the death of us all," Margaret added as she pushed Frank out of the front door.

"Don't you dare come back until you've found her?" Margret's words rang in his ears as he hurried down the cottage path. He had a good idea where Mary had gone, as her favorite bike was missing. Frank jumped on his own bicycle, which he had motorised since his Isle of Man accident. The smoking, noisy, little engine on the bike propelled him off to the Devil's Dyke.

He expected to find Mary in the hiding place in the gorse bushes at the top of the dyke. These were the same bushes he had always escaped to when life became too difficult. He had shown her the secret place when they had been on one of the long, slow walks together. Sure enough, he saw Mary's bike lying on its side on the slope of the dyke.

Mary was not surprised to see him. "Why does everyone hate us and call you a killer?" she said as he sat down next to her. "I just want all those horrid people to disappear and leave us alone." "You mustn't worry about other people. Most of them are just jealous and like seeing people like us in trouble," said Frank. "I'm really proud of you for standing up for me, but you shouldn't go around hitting people." As he spoke, Frank kissed the tight, black curls on Mary's head. He then put his arm around her and gave her a powerful hug and snuggled in close to her dad. But despite the reassurances he gave to his daughter, Frank knew he was a murderer. He had never told anyone about how he had shot that poor French boy in the war. He usually managed to forget that horror, but at that moment the memory felt raw. They remained there for five minutes without a word, comfortable together, before Mary said.

"Dad, are you ever worried or scared of anything?"
Frank thought for a moment before replying.
"No, I don't think I have ever been scared, but since you came along, I worry about you. I just want you to have a happy life."

Mary noticed tears in her father's eyes.
"You don't need to worry about me," she said with a weak smile. I'm Fearless Frank's daughter, remember?"
"You sure are," he said, hugging her tighter. "Now let's go back home together and face someone who is really scary…your mother." Mary giggled and gave him a long kiss on the cheek.

Frank didn't sleep at all the night before the inquest. It wasn't Margaret's light rhythmic snores that kept him awake. In fact, he found them somewhat comforting, as they reminded him of a distant motorcycle engine echoing through the mountains of the Isle of Man. With the grey, early morning light creeping along the bedroom ceiling, he wondered how he had gotten into such a mess. *Why does life start out so simple and suddenly become so complicated?* he wondered.

Suddenly feeling sorry for himself he envied his old schoolmates, who had been content to stay in the village and work the land all their lives.

Bloody cars, bloody motorbikes, bloody engines, he thought. *I wish they had never been invented. At least George Marshall had achieved his ambition, even if it did kill him. All I've got is a ruined knee to remind me of my failure.*

The sudden sound of Emily crying for her mother brought him back to reality. Frank knew that he had an exceedingly difficult and emotional day ahead.

The high-profile event was of international interest. The world's press had crammed themselves into the dark oak-paneled courtroom. Following the accident, sensationalist headlines covered the front pages of all the newspapers. Most of the bitter words of Victoria Marshall were quoted in full.

Ancestor of the famous Crusader Sir William Marshall killed at Brooklands race**course.**
George Marshall went out to battle to bring further honor to this illustrious family. A member of notorious killer's family has been implicated in the death.

This just one of the sensational Daily paper's headlines. Extensive coverage had been given to George's death, and some populist papers even showed a grainy, black, and white photograph of his body as it lay on the track. In contrast, the deaths of Albert and Madge Smith were given just a couple of sentences. They were nothing but a footnote at the end of each report.

Albert and Madge Smith (Albert had not officially changed their name to Smyth, so legally, they were still called Smith) had not been blessed with children. At the inquest, their four parents sat quietly alone in one corner.
Of course, the Marshall family were there in force. Silvia was sitting slightly apart as if to distance herself from the rest. Frank thought Silvia looked very pale and drawn, while he knew that Victoria Marshall's fixed scowl meant she had an overwhelming desire to see him officially blamed for the accident. The cacophony of murmured conversations and coughing silenced as Frank Cartland was called first to give his statement.

"Mr. Cartland. Will you give your explanation of the accident that caused the deaths of the Honorable George Marshall, Albert Smith and Madge Smith," said the coroner after Frank had been sworn in.

"Yes, sir. I had advised George Marshall that changing the axle ratio on his car would cause the engine to over rev and…"

"What's over, rev?" interrupted the coroner.

"Rev is short for revolutions per minute, sir. All engines have a safe limit," explained Frank quietly.

"Thank you. Carry on, Mr. Cartland."

"Mr. Marshall ignored my warning and told his mechanics to change the ratio. That is why the engine blew up, which then caused the accident."

Frank felt somewhat overawed by the experience, with the hostile Victoria Marshall staring at him. She had made sure that all their influential friends and the press knew that they thought George's death was Frank's fault.

"Did anyone hear you warn George Marshall?" asked the coroner.

"Yes, sir, his three mechanics stood beside the car and heard everything, but they were forced to do whatever George Marshall told them." "Thank you, Mr. Cartland, you may stand down," said the coroner.

Frank quickly returned to his seat, and Margaret gave him a weak smile He knew it was unfortunate that the three mechanics were the only witnesses to the argument with George about the dangers of changing the axle ratio.

Freddie O'Hare and two other well-known Brooklands drivers were then called to present their evidence. All confirmed that Frank was an exceptional engine builder and could not be held responsible for the disaster.

"Everyone knows that he's the best bloody engine builder at Brooklands," said Freddie in his usual colourful way.

"So, anyone who blames Frank for this accident is talking out of their arse. I saw the smoke coming from Marshall's car on that last lap. The bloody fool should have lifted his foot."

In fact, Freddie had been standing half a mile away and could not have noticed the smoke, but he thought that might help Frank.

"George Marshall couldn't drive a racing car to save his life," he added, unfortunately, which brought a snigger from the large group of newsmen. Next, the coroner called the three Marshall mechanics in turn. Under oath, each said that although they were close by, as Frank Cartland had said, when Mr. Marshall returned after his practice run. They had not heard the warning Frank had given their boss about the axle ratio.

"They are all lying. She's put them up to this," Frank interrupted. He stood and pointed at Victoria Marshall as the third mechanic nervously confirmed they had heard nothing.

"Sit down and keep quiet," the coroner told Frank sharply.

Before the hearing, Victoria Marshall had, as Frank guessed, instructed the mechanics to say they hadn't heard the argument. They were all employed on the family estate and couldn't afford to lose their jobs. The promise of some additional cash had ensured they answered as she insisted.

With no more witnesses to call, the coroner adjourned the court while considering his verdict. A worried Frank knew that it was going to be his word against a dead man, and although other drivers were there to support him, he feared the worst.

After the adjournment and an what felt like an exceptionally long wait for Frank, they were all called back into the courtroom. With the room in complete silence, the coroner stood up.

"Considering all the available evidence, The only conclusion I make is that this tragic event was an unfortunate accident," he said.

"Therefore, the verdict of this court for all three fatalities is death by misadventure."

It was a great relief to Frank and his supporters. He pushed through the crowd of reporters, without comment, and left the courtroom with a tearful Margaret by his side. Lady Victoria Marshall rushed over to him and, almost spitting into his face, said,

"Cartland, you haven't heard the end of this. We will make sure your life is a misery from now on."   With Margaret sobbing, the shouts of the Victoria Marshall and the world's press in his ears, Frank hurried to his old Morris 8 and drove slowly back to their Cambridgeshire home.

Before leaving for the inquest, Margaret told Frank she was expecting their fourth child. While back in Sefton Manor, Silvia Marshall had told no one that she was also pregnant.

Two young children waited in their respective homes for news of the day's events.

"What happened daddy, have they said the accident was your fault." Asked an anxious Mary as he opened the car door. She had been waiting next to the petrol pump for over an hour.

"No, my girl, no one has been blamed. Picking her he carried her into the cottage. "Now you must stop worrying. It is all over."

The following Margaret added.

"Don't kid yourself, Frank that Marshall woman is evil."

In Sefton Lodge William Marshall waited for his mother's return. He had watched his grandparents return to the Manor earlier and heard Victoria screaming at the servants while he stood in the porch of the Lodge. *Doesn't sound like the inquest went well.* He thought.
When Silva arrived looking pale, he assumed she was upset about the verdict.

"I've seen grandmother looking very unhappy, so I expect it was not the result you wanted." He said.
"That woman is an embarrassment, William. I'm sure Frank Cartland was not responsible, but your grandmother needs to blame anyone but your father."

227

George William Marshall's funeral was a noticeably quiet affair. There was none of the pomp and ceremony that had accompanied the funerals of his two brothers. After a private service in the family church, George was placed in the Marshall family crypt in Chichester cemetery, next to the remains of his brothers, Stuart and Matthew.
Despite protests from Victoria.

"The obsession with that badge and your encouragement is what had killed my son." She had shouted at Silvia when told that, on the coffin lid, George's Brooklands 120mph badge would be inset into the oak, alongside the Marshall coat of arms.

Lord John Marshall and Lady Victoria Marshall appeared pitiful as they stood silently inside the mausoleum. They had now lost all their children. The next day, the newspapers consent rated on pictures of the grieving widow Silvia, who looked stunning, if slightly overweight, in black.

Two people who'd had genuine affection for George, his chauffeur James Bird and his lover Hellen Dupery, did not attend the funeral. Hellen had deliberately stayed away from Brooklands on the day of George's record attempt.

She knew that the press would be more interested in her and Silvia's reactions than in praising George's efforts. She didn't want to take his moment of glory away from him.

Hellen heard the news of the accident in London that night when she read the headlines in the Evening Standard. She was genuinely upset, although it felt more like losing a faithful old dog than a soul mate. Like

Silvia, she knew that George was out of his depth and did feel some remorse that she had, in some way, contributed to his death. But his death allowed her to move on, something she had already decided she would have to do. To that end, only two days before the record attempt, she had made plans to take up the offer of a lover, Brooklands racing driver Baron von Rosenberg. He had invited her to stay at his castle in the Black Forest, only ten miles from the famous Nurburgring racetrack. She had decided that if the chance arose, she would remain in Germany.

Hellen had called into Frank's workshop earlier that day to give him the news. The well-used and now somewhat battered blue Bugatti sat alone and dusty at the back of the workshop.

"I am going away to Germany, Frankie, I don't think I will be racing Bleu Bebe again," she said.
"Very sorry to see you go, Miss Hellen," said Frank with concern on is face.

"What shall I do with this big pile of unpaid bills I've got for you." He opened the old desk drawer and pulled out a large handful of paper.

"I've been working on the old Bugatti these last two years, and you haven't paid me a bean yet."
Hellen gave Frank one of her famous big, warm smiles, as she always did when he asked for some payment.

"Oh, Frankie, I'm sorry. I have no money just now…but I know. Why don't you take Bleu Bebe as payment? She's yours to keep."

"I'm not sure she's worth much," said Frank, scratching his head. But I've grown fond of the old girl…so you've got a deal."

"Wonderful! I know she is in safe hands. Silvia told me how strong they are." exclaimed a happy Hellen giving him a wink. She clapped her hands together, gave her faithful Bugatti a final pat, and Frank a long, soft kiss on the cheek, then turned and glided out of the workshop without a backward glance. Red faced, and speak less Frank watched her go. That was the last time Frank saw Hellen Dupery.

James Bird had worked for the Marshall family all his life. His father had been the head coachman, and when he became too frail to continue, James had taken over the job. Social pressures ensured that all the major families had motorised transport as soon as they became reasonably reliable, and the Marshall family were no exception. Their first car arrived in April 1902, and James was their chauffeur from that day on.

James soon became an expert at curing the many mechanical ills of those early temperamental vehicles. Marshall family transport became his responsibility, from that first Panhard et Levassor touring car to the final second-hand Bentley.

Unlike anyone in George's family, James had encouraged him when he showed a genuine interest in driving and motors. On the day of George's death, James was at Sefton Manor repairing the old Bentley, which had broken down once again.

Local reporters descended on the manor with news of George's death long before the Marshall family arrived home. James was careful not to speak to them, but knowing George as he did, he was not surprised to learn that he had been killed.

He blamed Silvia, whom he hated, for how she had controlled and belittled George in recent years, just like his mother before her. Of course, he didn't share those thoughts with anyone.

Chapter Twenty-four

On a cool March morning in 1934, Margaret gave birth to a 6lb 2oz healthy boy with black curly hair in their bedroom at Ivy Cottage. They named their new arrival Peter Joseph Cartland.

Just 20 hours later, in a private room at Chichester General Hospital in Sussex, Silvia Marshall gave birth to a healthy, black-haired boy of a remarkably similar weight to Peter Cartland.

Of course, Lady Victoria Marshall was delighted to have another boy in the family, even though all other Marshall boys, for generations, had blond hair.
Anyway, she still had her blond-haired oldest grandson William to mold. He would carry on the family traditions and preserve the Marshall name.

Silvia was confident the father of her new son was not her late husband George. Fortunately, no one knew they hadn't had sex for at least two years before his death In fact, as soon as she knew she was pregnant, Silvia discovered that Frank Cartland was most likely the father. When she saw her new son's dark curly hair for the first time, she was sure of it. *I only went to give him a present, and I didn't expect one myself.* She thought, with some amusement.

Her new son she named David William Marshall, with Victoria Marshall's blessing, although that was of no importance to Silvia.

She was by now a very wealthy woman in her own right. She laughed to herself at the irony. She was now far wealthier than the snobbish older Marshall family.
Her father, with whom she had never been close, had died

of heart failure just a year after his grandson William was born. Simon Moncrieff left half of his fortune and the factories to his sons. He left the rest, including their three houses, to Silvia's mother. Alice Moncrieff had not lived long to spend and enjoy the money. Sadly, she committed suicide in 1927. The preceding years had not been kind to Alice. With the marriage of Silvia to George Marshall, she had naively expected to be accepted into the Marshall social scene.

She imagined being seen at Ascot, Wimbledon and Henley in the summer, skiing in Switzerland for Christmas, then spending three months in the South of France until England warmed again in spring. However, having an old family background was more important, especially to Victoria Marshall, than possessing a wealthy or notorious family history. Alice, with her northern accent, and lack of generations of family wealth didn't have the confidence to join in these traditional pleasures with the old families.

Once Victoria Marshall achieved her aim of marrying the family back into money, she ostracized Alice Moncrieff. Her forceful nature ensured that none of her social scenes welcomed Alice.

Disappointed and bored, Alice took many young lovers before and after Her husband died. In a social whirl of parties, drink, and drugs, she was quickly losing her looks and her health. She contracted syphilis when she reached forty but was in complete denial about the infection until it was far too late.

Silvia had little contact with her mother during this period. Alice's erratic behavior and excessive promiscuity became an embarrassment to her daughter.

When she eventually found out about her mother's condition, Alice was already on the edge of madness.

Silvia arranged for her mother to be sent to a private nursing home in Eastbourne, hoping for some cure.

It had been a year since William's christening, and the last time Silvia had seen her mother, so she eased her guilt by arranging a visit.
Silvia looked at this once beautiful woman with saddened shock and realised that the treatment wasn't working.

"How are you, Mother?" Silvia said, trying not to show how upset she was feeling.
Grabbing her arm and digging her nails painfully into her daughter's arm, Alice screamed into her face. "I need to get away. Take me home with you, take me home; the doctors here are all trying to kill me." Silvia pulled away, and a doctor rushed into sedate poor Alice.

Three purple bruises were already appearing on her right forearm as Silvia left the nursing home. She knew she would never revisit her mother.

One month later, on a cold and windy September morning, Alice walked out of the nursing home unnoticed by the staff. According to a dog-walking witness, she had found her way to Beachy Head and walked off the cliffs.

It was five days before Alice's body washed ashore, her body found two miles along the coast from the famous landmark. Although the mortuary assistant had done his best before Silvia went to identify her mother, some of the effects of five days of being bashed by rocks and considered fodder by crabs and small fish were still visible. The soft tissues and the eyes were the first to go, but thankfully, Alice's eyelids were closed when Silvia saw her mother for the final time.

Silvia's mother's death had a significant impact on her, although she felt more relief than sadness as she stood looking down at the white, sad shell.

Silvia knew that she owed this woman a great deal of thanks. Without her mother's ambition and forcefulness, she would probably now be married to an uncouth Northern lout instead of being one of the richest women in England.

Silvia had to organise the funeral herself and soon accepted how few real friends her mother had. Only eight people attended when Alice was buried in her hometown cemetery in Wakefield on a grey October day.

None of the Marshall family attended the funeral.

Chapter Twenty-five

William Marshall had grown into a strapping, handsome and self-confident young man. Although he had blond
The traumatic death of his father, which he had witnessed as a young boy, seemed to have had no lasting effect on him. He had witnessed the lack of affection between his mother and father as he was growing up. Just as George had been shown no love from his father, George had never demonstrated any fatherly love for William.

Even so, bearing witness to their father's death would have a long-lasting effect on many young boys, but William was made of sterner stuff. Her son's lack of emotional reaction had surprised his mother. Still, she was proud of, rather than worried by, his apparent detachment. William did not attend the inquest, although he had heard all the gossip at Sefton Manor. He knew his father had received little respect from the staff.

The day before the inquest, William had searched out James alone in one of the garages and went to talk to him.

"Please tell me James, why do you think my father crashed the Crusader at Brooklands." he asked.

"Sorry, Master William, but I didn't see the accident. You know I was here repairing the old Bentley," replied James.

"But you did know my father well, so you must have some idea why he crashed. Most of the family are sure it was Frank Cartland's fault."

"Your father was desperate to get his 120mph badge, so I'm sure he was trying very hard," said James diplomatically.

"Now, if you don't mind, please excuse me. Lord John wants the Bentley to take him to the station."

With great relief, James escaped further questioning from William. He didn't want his true thoughts to be known. He had gotten to know George's nature quite well over the years. He had always felt sorry for him but was convinced George would have be responsible for the accident.

After the inquest, William's grandmother turned her attention to him. When her twin sons were killed in the war, her previous indifference towards her only remaining son George had changed. She had devoted all her energies to finding him a wife. Now, she had a new project, and intended to take complete control of William's life.

When he reached the age of sixteen, she said, "You hold full responsibility for the future of the thousand-year Marshall dynasty, William." "I intend to help you fulfil your obligations."

Despite his youth, William clarified that he was not ready to be told how to run his life. Unlike his father, he was his own man.

Looking her directly in the eyes, something his father had never done, he replied.

"I know you mean well, grandmother, and I understand that when grandfather dies, I will be the eldest male Marshall, but I intend to decide my own future."

A shocked Victoria had no response. No one had dared to question her plans before.

Silvia was delighted to see William stand up to the old woman. She was proud that he had a mind of his own, unlike his late father.

William had also inherited her passion for fast, mechanical things, much to his grandmother's dismay. Victoria was horrified when she discovered that he had attended several Brooklands race meetings since his father had been killed. To make matters worse, William had fallen in love with the fascinating flying machines stationed and built there.

"Aren't they marvelous mother. It must be wonderful to have the freedom of the whole sky." He said as they watched two Tiger Moth's swooping around the sky over Brooklands.

"Next week, I will have my first flying lesson," William proudly announced to his mother as they drove home from the autumn members' meeting.

"Well, don't tell your grandmother, "Said Silvia smiling. "She is paranoid about your safety and would keep you in a glass case if she could."

William started his flying lessons in a Tiger Moth at the Brooklands track and quickly proved to have a natural ability for flying planes.

By the following spring, he had obtained his pilot license.

He called at Sefton Manor on his way home.
"Good evening, grandmother," he said as he gave Victoria a perfunctory kiss on the cheek. You may want to know that I have just obtained my pilot's license. I intend to join the Royal Air Force next year."   After a long silence she exclaimed "Why didn't you tell me you were flying? It's so dangerous. You are selfish, it's all your mother's fault. If your father was still alive, he wouldn't have allowed you to do it." *I'm sure he wouldn't have cared.* Thought William

"I didn't want to worry you or grandfather, so I decided to wait until I had qualified for my license before
I told you."

Standing now and red-faced Victoria spluttered. "You are due to go up to Oxford next year, so I will not allow you to join the RAF". There was an uneasy silence. But both knew she would have no say in the matter. Those days had gone.

"Well, now I must go and give Mother the good news," said William.

"I thought you would be pleased that I have told you first." He went outside, slid onto his motorbike, and rode the quarter of a mile down the drive to his home at the lodge.

Despite his grandmother's protests, William was determined to join the RAF as soon as possible.

Chapter Twenty-six

Four years had passed since the death of George Marshall.

These had been mainly uninspiring years for Frank Cartland, but they were quiet and happy for his family.

Having no knowledge of his other new son, David, Frank spent most of his time running the garage and enjoying time with his growing children, much to Margaret's satisfaction. By now, she had resigned herself to Mary remaining more interested in oil than perfume. *At least the other two are proper girls*, she thought.   It made her smile to know that the Marshall family had used their influence and money to ensure Frank was unwelcome almost anywhere motor racing took place. She was thankful to them; he had been given back to her.

A week after the inquest Frank had returned to his Brooklands shed to find Freddie waiting outside the locked door.

"Sorry old friend but it looks like the fucking committee have no balls. They have decided your continuing prescience here will bring unwelcome interest from the press. We all know that bitch has put them up to it."

"No big deal mate. I had decided to leave anyway. Too many bad memories at this place."

"All your stuff is in my shed, let's keep it there for now. Things may change in the future."

"Ok Freddie." Frank said to keep his friend happy but knew it unlikely he would be back at Brooklands. Frank had regretted missing much of his older children's early years and wanted to be around as Peter grew up. Unfortunately for Margaret, no matter how much Frank wanted to be an ordinary family man, he still had a more potent force inside him, bubbling to be let out once again.

Doctor Howard Jones turned up at the garage on an early April morning. He stopped with a screech of brakes, got out of his Morris 8 and rushed into the workshop brandishing a newspaper.

"It's all in here. You're cleared at last," Howard said excitedly to a surprised Frank.

"Slow down, Howard. What are you talking about?"

"Look what an old Marshall mechanic said to the papers. It's headlines on the back pages. He did hear you warning his boss about changing the axle ratio." "But why say that after all this time?"

"I don't know, but he has—see for yourself," said Howard, handing Frank the paper.

Sure enough, on the back page of the Daily Mirror, Frank read the headline.

Marshall mechanics lied at Brooklands inquest.

Alfie Barnes, George Marshall's chief mechanic on the day he was killed at Brooklands, now admits that he did hear the famous engine builder Frank Cartland warn his boss that changing the axle would be dangerous. None of the Marshall family was available for comment.

"That's all?" said Frank, throwing the paper down.

"The damage is already done… it won't change anything now."

But inside, he did feel a flutter of excitement. The racing passion was still burning deep within him.

On a beautiful, cloudless, late October day later that year, Frank packed the family into an old Austin 10 he had recently rebuilt. They drove the 3 miles up to Newmarket

Heath for a picnic and to watch the final horse races of the season.

Sitting on a blanket on the lush green turf, with the skylarks singing and the racehorses' hooves sounding like distant thunder, Frank reflected that although he had come a long way in 38 years, he was almost back where he had started. Sometimes, he felt he could feel those sharp cobbles digging into his body as his father beat him all those years ago.

He watched his three girls laughing and shouting as they ran up and down the green slopes of the Devil's Dyke, just as he and Joe used to do.

They were chasing their little wire-haired Terrier dog, Cassie, the granddaughter of his old friend, Spike.

Mary had undoubtedly inherited Frank's love for speed. Still a tomboy, she was more interested in Frank's joy in cars and engines than boys, and she spent many happy hours with him in the workshop.

Now a lovely 18-year-old, she was completely unaware of how her looks affected all the local lads. With Emily and Edith, both much more like their mother than him, chasing after their older sister, Frank was contented at that moment. He thought his life as it was now should be enough.

Looking down into the smiling, wide brown eyes of the four-year-old boy playing with the little tin car Frank had made him, he thought, just maybe, Peter could be the champion racing driver in the Cartland family. This was the one ambition that had eluded him.

They were all content as Frank drove home that afternoon, the girls singing in the back seat of the Morris, and Margaret happy in the seat next to him.

Her mood changed instantly when they turned the corner, and their garage came into view. Until this moment, she had been happy. Her life was finally settled with her family all around her. She wanted nothing more. But suddenly she could see her contentment was about to disrupted again.

Freddie O'Hare was waiting outside the garage. He was leaning against a sleek red racing MG Magnette K3. Pete Betts was admiring the car and filling petrol into it from one of Frank's yellow Shell petrol pumps.

What's that bastard doing here. He always brings trouble, thought Margaret as soon as she saw who it was. With a brief, wary "hello" to Margaret, Freddie then said to Frank,

"I'm going to Donington Park to watch these new German racing cars perform and thought you would like to come with me. We should celebrate now that bloody Marshall man has finally told the world the truth."

Of course, Frank had been reading about the German Mercedes and Auto Union cars in his monthly bible, Speed magazine. He knew that they were now dominating Grand Prix motor racing. The race at Donington Park had been due to run earlier in the year but had been cancelled due to Europe's uncertain political situation.

Recently, the British Prime Minister, Neville Chamberlain, had returned from meeting Adolf Hitler in Germany. All the papers were full of the headline "Peace in our Time" and photographs of Chamberlain waving a piece of paper they had both signed.

The International Donington Grand Prix has been rescheduled for the following weekend, 22nd October.

Frank also knew Chancellor Hitler had invested millions of Deutsche Marks in the German racing teams. With rising excitement, he thought *I can't miss the chance to see these incredible machines.*

"Just give me a minute, Freddie," he said as he followed his family who were already entering the cottage. Margaret had stormed into the kitchen, already noisily unpacking the picnic things. Frank with bright, excited eyes, looked pleadingly at her — like a little puppy begging for food.

"Do you mind if I go with him?" he asked.

"Of course, I mind, you bloody fool," Margaret snapped, "but I know you are going to follow that little sod anywhere. So why don't you just bugger off!"

Frank tried to give her a peck on the cheek, but she turned away. He entered their bedroom, grabbed a clean pair of socks, pants, and a shirt, and stuffed them into his old, brown leather travel bag. Mary was standing at the cottage door, blocking his way.

"I want to come with you."

"I'm sorry, Speedy," Frank replied, using his nickname for her. "I really need you here to look after the garage. Oh, and your mother and sisters," he added. Seeing the tears in her eyes, he said,

"You know I love you, Mary," he said before giving her a quick hug. Then he slipped into the passenger seat of the black MG. Freddie dropped the clutch, and Frank turned and shouted back to Mary.

"I promise I'll take you next time."

But Mary didn't hear his shout. The roar from the MG exhaust had drowned out his words.

243

Freddie and Frank happily disappeared up the road to Donington Park. Once again, they quickly left the mundane real world behind them.

Watching until the MG's noise had become just the sound of a distant, angry bee, Mary turned and stomped back into the cottage.

As Mary's younger sisters and little brother happily played a make-believe game around the kitchen table, she realised that she had never been as content as they were.

Thinking of her father, she whispered to herself, *I'm going to be just as selfish as you are as soon as possible. Let's see if you like that.*

Hearing Mary come back into the kitchen, Margaret shouted down from her bedroom,
"Mary, be a dear and make me a cup of tea. I'm having a lie down; I've got another headache."

Chapter Twenty seven

Frank had been wrong about the newspaper revelations. Alfie Barnes' change of tune certainly affected the Marshall family.

Barnes had been dismissed by Victoria Marshall as part of the family's cost-cutting exercise. He became very bitter when they evicted him from his cottage on the estate. The twenty pounds the Daily Mirror gave him for the story lasted only a short time, though. Drinking had always been Alfie's weakness.

Victoria stormed around the manor the day the story was printed, ensuring the staff said nothing to the posy of press standing at the gates.

"If anyone approaches you, make sure you all say Barnes was a drunken liar," she told them.

"If I hear anyone saying anything different, they will be fired."

Of course, William still wanted to know what had happened, but no one, not even his mother, would talk about it.

On one of his visits to Brooklands Flying Club, William had decided to call at one of the sheds used by Freddie O'Hare.
Nervously, he approached Freddie,

"Excuse me, Mr. O'Hare, but could you tell me where Frank Cartland has his garage?"

Freddie recognised this tall blond lad standing in front of him, and he was surprised by his politeness.
"Why should I tell you, you're a Marshall. Don't want you causing any more trouble for him," said Freddie, giving William a threatening look.

"Your fucking family has done enough damage to his life. They got him thrown out of here."

"I just want to know what really happened that day when my father died," said William, looking Freddie straight in the eye.

Freddie was impressed with this lad. *He thought he was much more his mother's son than his father's.*

"If I do give you his address, and I then find out that you caused that family more misery, I'll have your balls," said Freddie.

"I give you, my word. I've no intention of causing any trouble," replied William.

As Freddie gave William the address of Ivy Garage, he added. "Anyway, I can save you the trouble of speaking to Frank Cartland. Your old man died because he was a crap racing driver. It was no fault of Frank's."

William went home that evening and spoke to his mother.

"I intend to go and see Frank Cartland next week," he said.

"I'm not sure that's a good idea, but I will not try to stop you," said Silvia, surprised, "You can't change what has happened."

"I know that, but I would like to hear what he has to say. No one here will speak to me about the crash that killed father. Grandmother forbids the servants, and they are all afraid of her."

"It's also because we just want to forget about it," Silvia argued.

"Well, I'm going to listen to his version of the accident," said William determinedly.

Silvia, with some excitement, suddenly knew that the older generations of the Marshall family were gradually losing their influence.

Her son's actions were going to ensure that. The old generation were fading away. They were growing old and crumbling - just like their home, Sefton Manor, which was proving far too expensive for Lord Marshall to maintain.

In the previous year, he'd had to close the west wing of the house, and recently, part of a chimney had fallen, narrowly missing their one remaining gardener.
There was no Marshall money left for the necessary repairs. Dry rot had spread throughout the wing, and the roof leaked in numerous places. The reducing Marshall fortune had forced Lord John to slash the manor staff considerably over the preceding five years.

Only six servants remained to tend to his and Lady Victoria's needs, one of whom was the faithful old chauffeur, James. He now drove them slowly in the old, well-used Bentley, the Rolls Silver Ghost just a distant memory for James. It had been sold long ago, back in 1925.

After the inquest, the older Marshall clan had ostracized Silvia, just like her mother Alice. Victoria remained extremely bitter that Frank Cartland had escaped blame for her son's death at Brooklands. She really needed someone to be culpable.

She made sure that all her circle considered Silvia as guilty as Frank Cartland for forcing her son into taking the risks that killed him.

What Victoria and the rest thought did not matter to Silvia. She had William and now her younger son, David.   Silva was sure Victoria would be long dead before she could get her claws into David. She was confident that she and her boys would be the dominating forces in the Marshall family in the future.

The day after her father had left for Donington Park Mary was pottering in the workshop, feeling miserable. She was still angry with him for not taking her with him.

Six months earlier, he had been putting oil in the bores and turning over the Bugatti Type 35 engine. When she first noticed the Bugatti, Mary remembered hearing her mother's sharp words.

"What have you brought that old thing here for?" Were her angry words when she found out that her dad had taken the Bugatti instead of payment from Hellen Dupery for all the work he had done.

"You are so stupid, Frank Cartland," she had shouted.

"We need money, not that horrible, worthless, blue piece of junk."

Frank had ignored her harsh remarks, as he usually did these days. Mary knew he loved the car, and she could see why. With its beautiful shape, distinctive alloy wheels and the superb engineering of its mechanical parts, it was a work of art. Mary knew he intended to keep it, even though it would now be uncompetitive against more modern cars.

While he had been turning over the Bugatti engine, Frank had noticed his long-forgotten Triumph motorcycle under an old sheet in the corner *This is just the thing for Mary*, he thought.

Her father had wheeled the rusty and dusty old motorbike out into the yard.

"This is my old faithful Triumph; it hasn't been used for years, but if you can get it going, it's yours," Frank had said to her.

"Thanks, Dad, I'll soon have it sorted and running like new. That old, motorised bike is far too slow for me now, and anyway, it's always bloody well breaking down."
Frank had only said,
"Don't swear; you know your mother wouldn't like it."
Now, Mary remembered her boast as she struggled to remove the oily, old engine from the Triumph's frame. The old nuts and bolts, which had rusted in place over the years, were giving her problems. *This job is hard bloody work*, she thought.
Suddenly, the spanner slipped, and she smashed her hand hard onto the rough frame of the bike.
"Bugger, bugger!" she exclaimed as blood flowed from her skinned knuckles and cut finger. She was sucking her finger, trying to stop the flow of blood, when she heard the deep, throaty sound of a powerful motorbike nearby. Forgetting her damaged hand, she ran outside.
"Wow," she said, as the magnificent machine stopped before the petrol pumps.
With his helmet and goggles still on, the rider sat astride the bike, looking straight at her. He got off the bike and slowly removed his helmet and goggles. Mary saw a tall, strong-featured young man with, unfashionable, long blond hair standing silently by his motorbike.
For long moments they stood and looked at each other, surprise on both faces. The only sound the tick, tick of the cooling bike engine.
William Marshall had been intending to make this visit to Frank Cartland for a long time. Now that he was finally here, he was incredibly nervous, and not expected to find a beautiful young girl in oil-stained overalls at Frank's garage.

"Hello," he said quietly.

"Is this your bike?" asked Mary excitedly. She looked over the machine with envious eyes.

"Ye … Yes, it is," said William, unable to take his eyes off this unusual, lovely girl.

"I would like to speak to Frank Cartland. Is this his garage?"

Mary, still studying the motorbike, did not appear to hear him.

"It's a Brough Superior, isn't it? Which model?" Like her father before her, Mary immersed herself in the world of motor and motorcycling magazines. Her knowledge was not just casual, but deep-rooted. She knew this was the 'Rolls-Royce' of motorbikes. The Brough Superior, and that one had recently broken a record at Brooklands, reaching more than 143mph.

Surprised at her knowledge, William replied, "Yes, it's an SS680 overhead-valve, V twin." Eric Fernihough recently reached 143mph at Brooklands on a Brough."

Laughing, she said, "Actually, it was 143.39." She remembered the figure because her father had commented that 'George Marshall couldn't get his bloody great car to go that fast.'

Her eyes met his for the first time, a spark of intrigue flickering between them. Embarrassed, Mary broke the moment, leaving William with a lingering sense of curiosity.

"Sor...sorry, who did you say you are?"

"I'm William Marshall. I am hoping to speak to Frank Cartland."

It was Mary's turn to be surprised, and her happy mood immediately turned to anger.

"He's not here, and even if he was, he wouldn't want to see or speak to you," she said sharply, her words laced with anger.

"He's not going to be home for days, so you had better get back on that bloody machine and ride away from here."

Completely taken aback by her sudden change of mood, William said,

"I ... I just want to speak to him about my father, but I've got a letter in case he won't see me. I haven't come to cause any trouble."

William unzipped his brown leather jacket, pulled out an envelope and offered it to Mary.

"Would you please give this to him when he comes back?"

William stood with his arm outstretched, the envelope in his hand. Mary had stepped back, her hands on her hips and legs slightly apart, creating a clear distance between them. Slowly, William closed the gap, his arm still outstretched, offering the envelope.

Silently, Mary snatched the letter from his hand. Spots of her blood sprayed onto the envelope and the sleeve of Williams's leather jacket.

William gave her a weak smile and turned back to the Brough. He put his helmet back on, pulled down his goggles and kick-started the bike.

The deep, base sound as it burst into life caused Mary's knees to buckle. She held onto one of the petrol pumps for support.

A perplexed Mary watched the Brough Superior disappear down the lane. But it wasn't just the bike that had affected her. Her mother's bitter tales had filled her and her younger sisters' heads over the years. She had painted the Marshall family as evil, nasty, rich people who had ruined the Cartland family's lives.

Mary, of course, remembered the accident that killed George Marshall and caused her father so much trouble. Still, whenever she asked her father what had happened, the scar on his forehead would turn pink. He would get angry and refuse to talk about it. *That young man did not seem nasty at all,* she thought.

In fact, it was just the opposite. Meeting William Marshall produced emotions she had never experienced before.

Mary decided not to tell her mother about the visit. Fortunately, Margaret had taken the younger children to their grandfather's bakery for tea and cakes. Mary returned to the small garage office, sat at the old desk, and wrapped an old rag around her bleeding hand. Then she opened the letter.

William never needed an excuse to ride his motorbike. The fact that Burlham was almost 200 miles from his Sussex home was okay for him. With the Brough effortlessly eating the miles, he sped along the narrow, dusty lanes back south.

He was lost in the sensation of pure joy that the bike gave him with its' speed and power. With his heart beating with the pulse of the V twin engine, he felt like the bike and his body had merged into one living machine.

"Don't expect too much from him," Silvia warned him that morning when he announced he was going to see Frank Cartland.

"You know, since the inquest, your grandmother has been making his life hell."

When he returned to the lodge that evening, Silvia was waiting for him, anxious to know how Frank had reacted to the meeting. Hearing the Brough arrive home, she went out onto the gravel drive to greet William. "What did Frank Cartland say to you?" she asked the moment her son had taken off his helmet.

"He wasn't there. I left the letter with a pretty, blackhaired young woman in overalls."
Silvia immediately noticed the wistful look in her son's eyes.

"Who is the young woman?" she asked.

"I didn't have time to find out. She was extraordinary but got terribly angry when I told her who I was. She had been lovely and really interested in the Brough before I told her my name."

William's disappointment was palpable, his hopes dashed by Mary's unexpected reaction. Silva could sense his dejection.

"That sounds like Frank's daughter, Mary. I saw her once at Brooklands when she was a young girl. She was always just like him, mad about motors and covered in oil".

"I wish I'd had a chance to talk to her properly. I've never met a girl like her before," said William. He glanced down at the two dark spots on the sleeve of his jacket.

"I hope she gives him the letter." Pushing the bike into its garage, he added. "If I don't join the Royal Air Force, I have been thinking about applying for Cambridge University, so I'll call up there again in a few weeks."

"Do you think that's a good idea? You know all the Marshall boys have gone to Oxford University in the past.

Your grandmother will be upset if you go to Cambridge instead." said Silvia.

"Don't worry, I can handle her," William replied. Silvia couldn't help smiling. She knew when a man was smitten…she had experienced so many men chasing her over the years.

Chapter Twenty-eight

The German cars were sensational. Frank had never seen anything like them before. His hero, Silvio Bellini, drove one of the Auto Union cars. Bellini was a small Italian racing driver who had started racing motorcycles around the same time as Frank.

They had first met on the Isle of Man in 1925. After his TT race accident, Frank received a letter from Bellini offering his best wishes for a "rapido recupero". They lost touch after that, but Frank closely followed Silvio's racing progress in his motoring magazines, Speed and The Motor.

By the 1930s, Bellini had developed into one of the best racing drivers in the world. Arriving in the Donington Park paddock, Frank noticed his old Italian friend's orange jumper. He was talking to his German mechanics. Tentatively, Frank went over and reintroduced himself.

"Hello Silvio, I'm unsure if you remember me from your old motorcycling days?"

"Se mi remembers you, my old amico Frank" said Bellini in broken English. Shaking Frank's hand vigorously, he pulled on his red leather racing helmet to begin his practice laps.

"Come see me, tardi," he said. As he stepped into the great silver Auto Union cockpit, the car appeared to swallow him.

"Even the steering wheel looks bigger than him," said Freddie. "How the Hell does he manage to drive that thing?"

Silvio slammed the Auto Union into gear and fishtailed out onto the Donington Park circuit. "Bloody amazing," said Freddie, impressed, "I didn't know you were friends with racing royalty Fearless." "I haven't spoken to him for years," said a smiling Frank. He was really chuffed that Silvio Bellini had remembered him.

Bellini set the fastest laps at the start of practice, but then, when driving flat-out downhill through Hollywood bends, he was startled to find a large deer on the track. Even with his lightening reactions he could not avoid hitting it.

The silver Auto Union unfortunately killed the deer instantly, and Bellini damaged his ribs in the impact. Frank found him in the medical tent after practice. A young nurse was winding bandages around his ribs.

"I thought those antlers were going to spear you," said Frank.

"Se, bloody stupido animale, mi have antlers un trofeo," laughed Silvio.

"Are you going to be fit enough to race tomorrow?" questioned Frank,

"Naturalmente e vincerò," said the little Italian still laughing.

It was a bright sunny morning when, along with 60,000 other spectators, Frank and Freddie excitedly sat to watch the powerful and dramatic Silver Arrows.

This was the name given to all the Mercedes and Auto Union cars, as both manufacturers had painted their magnificent machines bright silver.

There were four Mercedes and three Auto Unions on the grid. The rest of the cars were mainly outdated English machines, the ERA and Frazer Nash cars being the quickest. Unfortunately, the fastest English car was over five seconds a lap slower than any sleek German machine.

The Duke of Kent started the 80-lap race.

As the Duke dropped the Union Jack, Silvio Bellini surged forward and immediately roared his Auto Union to the front in his bright orange sweater and red leather helmet. After 20 laps, the charging Bellini opened up a significant lead.

"Sod it," said a disappointed Frank the next time the car came past them. "It sounds like Silvio's engine is misfiring."

Sure enough, Bellini slowed, driving into the pits at the end of that lap to change plugs.

"He can't win now," said a disgusted Frank to Freddie as the silver Auto Union eventually flashed past them. Although the car was running strong again, they had dropped to fourth place. Frank and Freddie stood watching the spectacular race from the banking before the hairpin bend.

On the next lap, Bellini flew past them with the car almost sideways.

"He is driving like a madman," said Freddie. This made Frank smile, as coming from Freddie, that comment was funny. Freddie was the maddest driver he had ever seen.

Then, right in front of them, one of the English cars blew its engine, dropping oil all over the track.   "It must be one of your engines," joked Freddie, but before Frank had time to reply, Bellini arrived at full speed and hit the oil slick. In an instant, the silver Auto Union slid sideways, broadside across the grass, but with his arms twisting the steering wheel in a blur from lock to lock, somehow, the little man managed to wrestle the great car back onto the track. Load spontaneous applause erupted from the crowd. It was a moment of genius that all the spectators who had witnessed it would remember for the rest of their lives.

"That guy is superhuman," Frank roared.

All the spectators privileged to have seen Bellini in action that day knew they would never forget his uncanny skill. Setting the fastest lap time after time, Silvio Bellini was unstoppable. He re-took the lead on lap 67.

To grand celebrations, he went on to win. It was a magnificent victory. Frank could get near to speak to his old friend after the race with the world's press and wellwishers surrounding him. *What an amazing weekend,* he thought, as they sat in the MG waiting with the streams of cars attempting to leave the race track after the meeting. However, one thing that did disturb him, and many of the other English spectators, was the complete domination of the German machines.

Frank remembered reading about the German Mercedes team going to the 1914 French Grand Prix in force. They finished first, second and third, just as the German cars at the Donington Grand Prix had now dominated this race.

A few months after the 1914 French Grand Prix, Germany was at war with France and England.

Driving back, a strangely subdued Freddie said, "Bloody hell, Fearless, how are we going to build cars that can compete with those German monsters?" Frank had no answer.

Late that Sunday evening, Freddie dropped Frank off at home. Frank stood outside his garage long after the snarling MG had disappeared. He smoked a final Woodbine as he leaned against one of his Shell petrol pumps.

With his ears still ringing from the shattering noise of the V12 German engines, he knew he needed to be immersed, once again, in the exciting, intoxicating world of motor racing.

He couldn't help it. This desire for speed was in his blood.

It was 1938, and events in Europe were already taking the world on a terrifying, unstoppable course. Frank Cartland and Silvia Marshall had no idea that the consequences of these events would ensure that they would have little control over their own, or their families' futures.

Bibliography

Adventurers Fen: E.A.R. Ennion

Brooklands to Goodwood; Rodney Walkerley

Brooklands Volume 1 W.Boddy

Bugatti Queen: Miranda Seymour

Early one Morning: Robert Ryan

Fast Women: John Bullock

My Lifetime in Motorsport: Sammy Davies

Norton Motorcycles: Jim Reynolds

The British at Le Mans : Ian Wagstaff

The Donington Grand Prix: Dave Fern

The History of Motor Racing: W. Boddy

The Le Mans 24 Hours: David Hodges

The Roaring Twenties: Cyril Posthumus

The Story of the T. T: G.S. Davison

Pre-view
Deadly Obsessions
Part 2
The Triumphs and the Tragedies
Now available

    They were desperately choking in the cloying dust rising from the chalky rubble. Men and women continued lifting the rubble and crushed beams for hours, but there was still no sign of Franks' wife or daughter. The German Doodlebug had arrived over Burlham at 10.45 that morning.

    Gravedigger Harry Williams had dropped his spade and looked up when he heard the harsh mechanical clatter above his head. Suddenly, the noise stopped.

    He watched in horror as the now silent, deadly machine travelled over his head. It was losing height rapidly, and he could see it heading straight down towards the village school.

    As the grey flying bomb passed St Mary's church, Harry could hear the high-pitched laughter of the children in the playground enjoying their morning break time. ...

Deadly Obsessions
Part 3
The Victor and the Vanquished

Will be available soon…
If you would like to go onto the email list to be advised the moment part three becomes available, please go to
www.racingbooks.org

Printed in Dunstable, United Kingdom

65924847R00157